GAMES
REAL ESTATE
AGENTS
PLAY

BY

THEODORE IVERSEN

REPRODUCTION INFORMATION

Copyright
1992
Theodore Dennis Iversen

Library of Congress Cataloging-In-Publication Data

Iversen, Theodore Dennis

GAMES REAL ESTATE AGENTS PLAY

1. Real Estate
2. Business

I. Title

92-091099

ISBN 0-9635259-1-3

Printed in the United States of America

ABOUT THE AUTHOR

Theodore Iversen holds a Master's Degree in Business Administration, specializing in Finance, from the University of Southern California. He also holds a Bachelor of the Arts Degree, specializing in English Literature, from the University of California, Los Angeles.

Mr. Iversen, a licensed real estate agent in the state of California, has spent ten years researching and writing this book. Some of the case examples are personal experiences, giving rise to the book's concept.

CONTENTS

DEDICATION

To all the Lambs,

Trusting,

Unsuspecting,

Ready to be shorn.

God help us all!

CHAPTER 1

THREE B's

His name was George F. Babbitt, and...he was nimble

in the calling of selling of houses

for more than people could afford to pay.

- Sinclair Lewis, *Babbitt* (1922)

BASIS

The purpose of this book is three-fold:

>   1. To educate and to protect consumers from the shady tactics and games that are played every day--every minute--by many people in real estate;

>   2. To demonstrate to real estate agents that honesty, hard work, good customer service, and a dedication to helping people and fellow workers results in higher earnings, self-fulfillment and greater esteem;

>   3. To illustrate to the residential real estate industry the most serious problems that undermine consumer confidence, and to provide solutions for rectifying these problems.

This book culminates a decade of research. The case examples presented here are real. This book was written with input from veteran brokers, bankers, developers, sales agents, buyers and sellers--all to provide you with the necessary well-rounded perspective. Names have been changed in order to maintain the privacy of the many contributors.

From the thousands of cases that were collected and analyzed and from seeing a multitude of people in the business come and go, several principles have been noted. The principles written in these pages are timeless; they apply to real estate agents fifty years ago, today, and fifty years beyond tomorrow.

This is a book about *markets, marketing and human behavior.*

May this shared knowledge benefit and protect you throughout your lifetime.

BACKGROUND

Residential real estate agents are "dogged" by an image problem. The business is perceived skeptically by many Americans. Finding a "good agent" has become as troublesome as finding the proverbial "honest contractor" or auto mechanic. How can one be located who will not take advantage of a person in need?

Random samplings of calls to neighborhoods across the country indicate that the American public has grown extremely wary. A large percentage of people terminate the conversation when someone identifies one's self as a "real estate agent." Follow-up calls reveal that these people believe the industry to be shoddy, full of liars, cheats, crooks and swindlers. What has brought on this sad state of affairs?

There are many fine agents available. They suffer because of the unscrupulous individuals who have given the business a bad reputation. Who are the "bad apples"? How can you spot them and recognize their tricks?

While the tone in parts of this book might seem harsh, this ire is directed at the people who play the games of deception. They do not represent the majority of agents in the industry.

But in these pages, you will meet innocent people who have been "thrown into the street" because they placed their trust in some kind, sweet-talking individual.

And you will also meet superstars--*Rainmakers*--honest and upright seasoned professionals who serve clients with a sincere desire to help mankind, who are reliable, courteous, trustworthy, who look out for your welfare in a real estate transaction.

Rainmakers are rewarded with a higher level of success and more earnings than others in the business, enjoying the advantage of an outstanding community reputation, more referrals, unsurpassed esteem in the eyes of colleagues, and above all, self-fulfillment.

This book is written so that you may find or emulate the *Rainmakers*, rather than becoming one of the many "victims" who share their stories in successive pages...

BLUEPRINT

The chapter sequence is designed to maximize your understanding of the residential real estate industry as seen from points of view of agents, buyers and sellers. The chapters are summarized below, in order:

"In Theory..." sets up a "straw-agent," i.e., a definition of an agent and what function the individual serves in society. Even if you are a professional investor, it is good to review this short chapter for the image that it conjures.

"In Reality..." shows how very powerful forces are at odds with the theory: the forces of ambition, greed and survival. The things that an agent learns in real estate school do not translate well to the real world when one is starving. Who enters the real estate field? What are the backgrounds? Is the training appropriate?

"Myths" demonstrates how reality on the street conflicts with the theory. You learn that popular ideas have become manifest erroneously, largely due to the general public's desire for truth--and you meet hungry agents who gladly step-in and dispense a substitute. Like the myths of the *MEGA-AGENT* or the *MEGA-FIRM*. Or "location-location-location." Or the "benefits" of open houses. When one repeats falsehoods often enough, some people come to accept the stories as facts. As long as the myths help sell properties...

"The Games" continues the agent's stray from the Garden of Eden as described in the theory. Footloose and fancy-free, a multitude of tactics are unleashed that are designed to move money out of a client's pocket. Such as the "I Have a Buyer" and the "Our Agency" routines. Or the "Old Shoe" and "Fab Five" techniques. If you are not aware of these subtle games, you too may fall.

These myths and games damage the industry. The general public is rarely aware of them when they happen. Sometimes newspapers publish the stories, and the public dismisses these occurrences as isolated instances.

But these "isolated instances" occur day-in, day-out, year-in, year-out. And if you put many similar stories together, and many stories into principles, then the resulting advice shows you how to recognize the deceptive tricks of the "bad apples" who want nothing more than to take a client's money--regardless of the consequences to the client.

For this reason, you are given *many* case examples in this book which occur *every day* in the business in order to support the principles, thus broadening your knowledge. Understanding what is happening and how it affects you in a real estate transaction is of paramount importance...

"The Housing Market?" analyzes the forces that enable homes to sell, separating fact from fiction. Not simply abstract theories of supply and demand. Straightforward information relevant to your home, your block--such as why one home can sell when one next to it cannot. Things that you can *apply*. Supply and demand curves are wonderful, but they usually only describe static conditions at a given point in time. It is better to anticipate where markets are moving so that you don't get left behind.

"Buyer Beware" does more than tell you about how to pre-qualify yourself or which homes to avoid. It also tells you about negotiations. About a seller's psychology. About agents who don't care which house you buy as long as you buy one from them, and how to spot their tactics. About how you, as an investor, can lose a lot of money by not using one simple technique. Every seller should read this chapter to learn how buyers fall prey to bad advice and the pitfalls in the marketplace.

"Seller Beware" is recommended reading for everybody. Much time and hope can be wasted on phony leads and solicitations from agents. What do the phone calls mean? What is behind them? Why do they discourage sellers? Should you sell it yourself? How should your home appear on paper? Did your home sell too quickly? Or why didn't it sell? This chapter gives buyers insight into the frustrations of sellers. And understanding a seller's plight is a buyer's key to improving communication and negotiations.

"Attributes of Rainmakers" should be read after you have finished all of the previous material. By then you will have seen the games and learned the scams. This chapter shares the traits and habits of successful people in the business who were tracked over a ten-year period, presenting accurate images of what to look for in an agent, such as how to measure competence, how to gauge attitude, how to measure productivity... And also which agents may not be best-suited to your needs... You shouldn't just pick up the phone or listen to the advice of a friend. If you do this, you may as well dial a Las Vegas Casino... with credit card handy...

"Toward Cleaning the Industry" presents some startling cases in order to recommend the most critical steps required to restore the credibility of the residential real estate industry. Realty boards have attempted to regulate ethics and behavior for many years to little avail. These boards are usually comprised of the best people who set shining examples. Unfortunately, without mandating the recommendations contained here, they will continue to be unsuccessful in their efforts to raise overall public esteem.

"Epilogue" recaps the book and offers a futuristic vision of possible real estate transactions based on trends in emerging technologies. This vision is both idealistic and mechanistic--where most of today's problems are solved...

CHAPTER 2

IN

THEORY...

One generation passeth away,

and another generation cometh;

But the earth abideth forever.

- Old Testament, *Ecclesiastes, i 4*

TERMINOLOGY

To begin, let's set our terms straight. Residential real estate salespeople are primarily divided into the following two categories:

First, a *broker* is a person who is licensed to practice real estate by the state. The broker usually has extensive experience in the business and has passed an exam equivalent in difficulty to the bar exam for lawyers. If the broker is a member of the National Association of Realtors (NAR)--as many are--then the broker is designated as a *realtor*.

Second, the broker may employ a *sales agent* or *sales associate* who is also licensed by the state. The licensing requirements are much easier for new sales agents, and the newcomers are not required to have any experience in the industry. The sales agent works under the supervision of the seasoned broker. And if the sales agent is a member of the NAR--as many are--then the agent is designated as a *realtor associate*.

For the purpose of this text you will only see the words "broker" or "agent/ sales agent." In common parlance, this simply differentiates between the "employer" and the "employee," respectively. (The sales agent is technically an "independent contractor" who does not possess employee status.)

Most of the case examples in this book describe the dealings of people with only a sales agent designation. All of them were members of the NAR. Sales agents happen to be the majority of people in the residential real estate industry that you will ever meet.

Both brokers and agents are capable of the chicanery depicted in this book. Consumers usually don't care about the formal titles of those who dupe them. It is less important to learn the designation of someone playing duplicitous games than to recognize the games and their ramifications.

In any case, a broker or sales associate serves in the capacity as an intermediary who facilitates an exchange in the marketplace between buyers and sellers. For this service, a commission is paid.

But what are the formal controls which supposedly govern behavior and prevent the games that real estate agents play? To begin answering this question, let us first examine the codes of conduct pledged by the majority of real estate agents that you will encounter...

THE MODEL

The strength of any nation depends upon its peoples' wise and diligent use of its resources. The land provides the food, the farms, the jobs, the housing, the cities, the industries--the very core of the institutions and of civilization.

Because real estate agents are entrusted with transactions involving the land, a set of moral and social obligations beyond those of ordinary commerce should govern their behavior, according to the industry's Code of Ethics.

The Code of Ethics deems that all people in real estate should strive to become pillars of their communities. They should:

> Be informed on all matters concerning real estate in order to contribute responsibly to the public good;

> Eradicate any negative personal behaviors or practices of fellow agents that discredit the industry;

> Share their knowledge and time willingly with associates for the overall benefit of the public--for as the standards of the industry improve so will society.

Coupled with these lofty aspirations are obligations that--if not followed--are grounds for disciplinary action, such as:

> Place the client's needs before one's own;

> Conduct business so that one does not discredit or take unfair advantage of one's associates; do not knowingly make false or misleading statements about competitors;

> Receive compensation only from fully disclosed sources;

> Represent property and facts in a transaction truthfully, avoiding exaggeration or concealment of information;

> Avoid discrimination against anyone with regard to race, color or creed;

> Treat all parties in a transaction fairly;

> Provide and maintain competent service;

Disclose any hidden or contemplated interest in a transaction in which one can benefit, either by ownership or by referral of services;

Resolve any disputes with fellow members through arbitration by a body of peers, and supply these peers with all pertinent information, assisting in the arbitration process;

Recommend legal counsel or other professional assistance to those who need it rather than render a personal opinion outside one's scope of expertise;

Maintain accurate and appropriate books and records. Do not commingle personal and client funds;

Maintain truth in advertising;

Avoid interfering with any relationship an associate may have with a client;

Express all real estate commitments in writing, distributing copies to all involved parties;

Utilize the services of fellow associates when it is in the best interest of the client.

These tenets constitute the most essential, and can be summed by the Golden Rule: "Do unto others as you would have others do unto you."

This model serves as the cornerstone of the industry. One might wonder what mechanisms are in place to enforce this behavior.

Is the industry flawed--providing an ineffective means to protect you, the consumer? Are these guidelines mere platitudes without "teeth"? Is the industry structured to further the interests of its members, serving less the public good and more the private purse?

Let us step down from this mountain and travel through the world of residential real estate, answering all of these questions...

CHAPTER 3

IN

REALITY...

Whenever anyone says "theoretically,"

they mean "not really."

- Dave Parnas

WHAT DO THEY TEACH IN REAL ESTATE SCHOOLS?

Facts. Facts. Facts. Facts. Facts. Facts. Facts. Facts. Facts. Facts...

What have you learned from the preceding sentence? Congratulations! You passed the sales exam! You are now qualified to sell real estate. Actual examples of questions that are taught by the schools to regurgitate on the exam are:

1. As a motive to buy, the financial enhancement in purchasing a home would be:

   a.   primary;
   b.   secondary;
   c.   absolute;
   d.   irrelevant.

2. Which of the following is the difference between a mechanic and a judgment lien:

   a.   a mechanic's lien is a statutory lien;
   b.   a mechanic's lien may not be enforceable after some time;
   c.   a judgment must be recorded to become effective;
   d.   a judgment lien is an involuntary lien.

3. The broker must maintain a copy of a listing agreement for a period of:

   a.   7 years;
   b.   4 years;
   c.   1 year;
   d.   5 years.

4. Many federal and state laws prevent discrimination. In which year did the Federal Civil Rights Act become effective?

   a.   1936;
   b.   1972;
   c.   1959;
   d.   1968.

The point here is that little, if any, of this information will teach you how to become a better real estate professional. It will not teach you how to become successful. It will not teach you about the most important factor in the business: customer service.

Great men like Henry Ford did not carry around books of facts. He hired an army of accountants, engineers and lawyers. He worked through people, focusing on customers' needs.

Many people use real estate schools and take real estate exams, hoping that passing will enable a sure-fire path to riches and success.

But the "school of hard knocks" on the street offers a different reality.

Someone who is hungry has incentive to abandon this information quickly and develop a different set of skills.

Facts are readily forgotten. Their mastery simply constitutes a deceptive "rite of passage" into the real estate industry.

WHO TAKES THE REAL ESTATE EXAMS?

Because of the relatively easy requirements for obtaining a real estate sales license, on any given day you often find the following social stratification of people taking the sales exam:

10%	Professionals;
10%	Retirees;
80%	Non-professionals changing trades, recent high-school graduates, homemakers, and people without much business training.

These percentages are reasonably consistent as demonstrated by samplings of enrollments at real estate schools and of people exiting the exams. There is really only one critical question to be asked regarding these percentages: do the backgrounds contribute favorably to success?

The industry has studied its successful agents, finding that there is a direct correlation between education and success. This is not the only crucial factor, of course. An educated person who is dishonest is extremely dangerous, and is doomed to failure after wrecking many people's lives.

Consumers want agents who have integrity and are hard working, especially since they are handling such a substantial and consequential transaction.

Some very fine people have entered the industry and have succeeded, regardless of educational background. Through sheer determination, these individuals have learned about business from extracurricular studying, seminars, tapes, etc. Such people are the exception, however.

How many of the people taking the sales exams have formal business training? Should they first be skilled in finance, economics, accounting, marketing...especially if they are going to recommend to sell a home and buy another because, as many often say, it "makes economic sense..."? For whom?

Instead, most of the newcomers train with "veterans" who have been fortunate to have made good money in a short period of time during a rising market, having incentive to weather the business in its downcycles. But, like these newcomers, many of the "old timers" have also had no formal business training. They learned by "the ropes" or through "on the job training," which all too often means using deceptive sales tactics on clients.

Everyone in real estate requires a broad network of fellow sales agents, escrow agents, advertising staff, accountants, credit analysts, loan and mortgage brokers, economists, contractors, tax specialists...a business network where a business and public relations background are most helpful. There should be enough cross-training in order for everyone to know the common terms, and one's limitations...

Rather, real estate is popularly conceived as a "get-rich-quick" scheme which almost anyone can master. For this reason, many people without adequate training enter the industry, cause a little damage, get discouraged and drop out when they learn how inaccurate and whimsical this "easy-money" notion can be--especially in slow markets. Meanwhile, the cycle repeats and more new people enter, making life harder for the people who remain...

Real estate requires a minimum of 8-10 hours of hard, organized, dedicated effort each and every day in order to obtain true professional status. To stay sharp. To obtain accurate knowledge. To hone one's skills. To maintain an edge. To be a master over one's transactions, client relations, new business development, and knowledge of people and events in the industry.

Instead, perhaps someone with no business background wants a part-time job. Maybe the real estate market has been very strong in the area recently. A friend has been selling real estate part-time and making a lot of money. Lately. In fact, the friend is now working <u>full-time</u>. Lately. The newcomer likes the flexibility that real estate offers and enters the business. The market suddenly sours. The new agent sells two houses, then quits. The friend resumes part-time status. Business is slow.

Fortunately, the broker who temporarily employed this new agent has "Errors and Omissions" Insurance: a family who bought one of the newcomer's houses is protected. The new agent neglected to tell the family that the information on the property description sheet only contains approximations. A "bedroom" that has no closet is really a den. A closet is now being built, thanks to the insurance. When business picks up, the new agent will be back, possibly knocking on your door...

Unfortunately, this common illustration does not just happen with new agents. It also happens to "veterans" who continually exit and re-enter the business, accruing "years of experience..."

A DAY IN THE LIFE...

A day in the life of a residential real estate agent follows, including the typical ups and downs.

6:00 a.m. Rise. Workout. Shower. Prep. All with National Public Radio blaring in the background.

7:30 Breakfast meeting with a client. Discuss the marketing plan for a home valued at $2.5 million. Client wants extra guaranteed "freebies," e.g., front page layout on Sunday supplement, open houses every Sunday... Client tries to grind commission down from 6% to 4% to equal the same as a competing firm. Drive to office. Already a headache! Feels like a great day!

9:00 Office meeting begins. Glance at this morning's 12 phone messages. One is from escrow: deal may be falling out. One is from a loan officer: potential clients cannot qualify for the home they want to buy. One is from a client: wants name of a reliable contractor. Another is from a client: wants to change 1:30 p.m. appointment to 2:30. Another client: wants to reschedule 4:00 p.m. showing for 2:00 p.m. Another client: wants the name of a good handyman. An agent: bringing in an offer on a listing; would like to present it tonight. Another agent: can you recommend a good home inspector? Another agent: also bringing an offer on the same house! Another client: calling about a listing. Another client: received brochure in the mail--would like to talk. Last call: personal. Looks like a slow day... Who's paying attention to this meeting anyway? Who wants to ask sellers to be more "realistic"? Inventory of unsold homes has increased by 35% in the last six months while home prices have tumbled 10%. How "realistic" should sellers be?

9:55 Meeting is over. Two more messages. Phone escrow: ASAP. Phone a seller: ASAP. Try to work in office. Three agents stop by. Chit-chat. Speak to head broker regarding 4% commission request. Am reminded that people don't work for free in this office.

10:20 Glance at clock and notice that last 1 1/2 hours have not been too productive. Prepare for caravan.

10:25 Retreat to safety of car. Begin driving to our office's open houses. Begin returning phone calls. Call two agents with presentations. Leave messages. Call seller for presentation meeting. Leave a message. More phone: escrow--deal fell out; buyer submitted cancellation instructions due to poor home inspection (i.e., really bought another house--home inspection info can always be negotiated). Seller call: very upset--shouting--an agent showed the house this morning without making an appointment--and saw wife exiting shower naked and let dog out. Commiserate. Promise to "give the agent hell."

10:45 Pull up to first house. It barks. The agent overpriced it. Will be a bad rep for our firm. Wish her luck...

10:49 Back in car. Continue calls. Move 4:30 appointment to 2:00. Let 1:30 appointment slide until Saturday. Why? The 4:30 client has a fat wallet and is in a hurry to buy.

11:02 Next house. Not bad! Lot's of charm for $399,000. Briefly discuss details and terms with agent.

11:10 Back in car. Annotate that the Johnsons must see this house. It suits their needs perfectly. Better idea: phone Mrs. Johnson. Please come and see the home... Agent is waiting, house is open...

11:20 Next house. Great. Will try to keep it in mind.

11:25 Next house. It also barks. But, it's undervalued. Annotate it for an investor as a potential purchase.

11:38 Next house. Great. Will try to keep it in mind.

11:45 Next house. Great. Will try to keep it in mind.

11:55 Next house. Great. Will try to keep it in mind.

12:08 Next house. Great. Will try to keep it in mind.

12:15 Next house. Great. Will try to keep it in mind.

12:22 Continue phoning seller. She will be available this evening at 7:00 p.m. for the presentations. Phone agents. Leave one message. The other cannot meet at 7:00. Can make it 7:30? Take a personal call: you are loved! That helps!

12:30 Back at the office. Most people out. Good. Can now get some work done...

Close office door. Pull food out of refrigerator. Back to phone. Call investor: discuss undervalued home. Suggest buying it. He wants to wait and see whether prices keep falling...

Phone client: recommend contractor. Phone client: recommend handyman. Phone client: recommend home inspector.

Phone agent: recommend another line of work! How dare he walk in on my client when she was in the shower! And didn't he see the dog! What if the poor animal ran into the street and were hurt? The agent tries to make a joke out of the situation. Thank you. Appreciate your sense of humor. Hang up. Talk about crass!

Some "free" time. Read paper. Notice that section of town with this morning's undervalued home is being renamed...

Immediately call investor. Still wants to wait. A knock on the door: more phone messages. New temporary secretary had misplaced them...sorry for the delay... Mrs. Johnson: saw the home. Likes it. Wants to think about it. Agent: offer that was coming in tonight has been delayed. Still working on buyer. Phone the seller: reschedule 7:00 p.m. appointment for 7:30.

1:34 Open office door. Chit-chat with agents. Then, leave for appointment.

2:00 Pickup family. The kids are noisy in the back seat. Show neighborhood. Show house. He likes it! She's not sure Can the kitchen appliances be updated? Can another closet be added somehow in the master bedroom? Everything is negotiable. Will price it out. Drive to next home. Pickup ice-cream on the way. It's a hot day! Next house is great, but they like the floorplan of the last house slightly more. Husband preferred last house. Wife finally decides on last one also. Of fifteen homes shown this week in their price range, they prefer the last home. Please price-out closets and appliances, and they will write an offer adjusting for these items.

4:10 Drop off family. As they leave, notice ice cream on the back seat...

Call office. Four messages. Agent with undervalued home phoned: house is sold! Recommends submitting a backup offer if the investor is interested... This morning's client: decided to go with other firm--they agreed to a 4 1/2% commission. Good luck--we'll talk in a few months... Irate seller: apologizes for overreacting about wife & dog. Escrow: another deal may be falling out.

Oh well... Mind wanders in traffic... Reflect on the virtues of never drinking. Not only stay sober through all this fun, but the bar bill would probably exceed the phone bill...

4:42 Back home. Change. Scan Wall Street Journal. Scan local business paper. Eat. Nap. Shower. Dress.

6:00 Phone new client regarding brochure: arrange for an appointment tomorrow. Jump on computer. Obtain latest "sold" data for 7:30 p.m. appointment. Check phone messages. Investor wants to put in an offer on the undervalued home. Too late! Also received five inquiries on a newspaper ad. Will tend to those later.

6:47 Leave for 7:30 appointment.

7:18 Arrive at 7:30 appointment. Other agent has arrived early and is already inside the home. Great. Trying to get "chummy" with someone else's client...? Oh well, offer is too low. Buyer's client wants to steal it. Buyer's agent talks about selling-price trends. Apologizes for buyer--wants a counteroffer--believes she can "talk-up" the buyer. Please counter!

Seller feels offended. So, spend 20 minutes talking about the psychology of real estate. About tacky buyers with crummy first offers. About tacky agents who show up too early... Seller feels better. Write a counteroffer.

9:58 Arrive back home. Call five ad inquiries. Leave two messages. Describe home to three people. Set showing appointment with one. Check messages. Home inspector: thank you for the referral. Mrs. Johnson: can we see some more homes this Sunday? Personal: please call!

11:12 Lights out! The end of another slow day...

PRIORITIES

For many new real estate agents, an incorrect set of priorities takes precedence over the innumerable facts and semi-useful knowledge quickly learned, quickly forgotten, from initial studies for the real estate exam.

Rainmakers tell agents to concentrate on such things as "consistency" and "the priorities of the seller or buyer." The new agent tries to focus on these. After a short period of starvation or roller-coaster pay periods, the new agent's priorities quickly change from the client's to the agent's. Here are the client's:

Client's Priorities (Seller)

1. Sell the home
2. Keep the house in "show condition"
3. Aggressively advertise--in papers, flyers, signs...
4. Regularly hold open houses
5. Boldly market--to other agents

Client's Priorities (Buyer)

1. Find the perfect home
2. Get a great deal
3. Obtain favorable financing
4. Obtain favorable terms & conditions
5. Move-in on time

These priorities may not be in the order of every person, but random surveys demonstrate that they are consistently on nearly every person's list. Many agents lose sight of these priorities, which contain the essence of fine customer service. Instead, compare them to the agent's, below:

Agent's Priorities

1. Commission
2. Commission
3. Commission
4. Commission
5. Keep the broker reasonably happy

Survival on the street dictates this set of priorities. It is the first thing one learns as a new, hungry agent, and the last thing one ever forgets...

THE "HAVES" AND THE "HAVE-NOTS"

Like most businesses, real estate contains a "caste system": the privileged and the underprivileged. They are known as the "broker" and the "sales agent," respectively. The differences between them are given below:

Broker:

- owns the company
- firm usually carries the broker's name
- broker's name is the primary one on any contract, carrying the full responsibility and liability
- broker maintains a fiduciary agreement with the client
- broker has usually been in business for many years
- has passed an exam equivalent to the bar exam for lawyer's
- has the knowledge (extensive)
- has the training (extensive)
- has the experience (extensive)
- has the reputation (earned over many years)
- has the connections
- is usually too busy to meet with you personally
- is usually an "administrative type"
- determines policy
- makes the priorities
- sets the company goals
- assigns the tasks
- distributes the sales goals
- receives all of the commission--then pays the sales agent
- is the "employer"

Sales Agent:

- has passed a reasonably easy entrance exam
- is almost always your connection with the broker
- is usually an "unpaid slave" of the broker
- is like an "employee," but of lesser status
- is usually "broke" after the first six months of training

Think of the broker as the sky and the agent as the deep blue sea. Between the two is every agent that you deal with, from novice to the most advanced.

Does tenure equate to success in the business?

Case example 1345: Seller A listed his home four times over a period of two years with several seasoned agents. Their combined experience totaled 46 years. The fifth time Seller A used an agent with only two years of experience. She sold the home quickly. And the market was declining all during this time.

What contributed to the agent's success?

She had an extensive business background, strong networking skills, and a superior marketing strategy.

She was a *Rainmaker*...

CHAPTER 4

MYTHS

The mighty pyramids of stone

That wedge-like cleave the desert airs,

When nearer seen, and better known,

Are but gigantic flights of stairs.

- Longfellow, *The Ladder of St. Augustine*

TRUTH IN ADVERTISING

Advertisements for homes in the real estate industry are not designed to sell houses. They are designed to:

a)   Generate leads;

b)   Promote the company.

Because of this focus, there is a vast difference between an ad for a house and ads for other types of products.

For example, consider an ad designed to sell a sofa. Usually the ad contains a picture of a sofa and the price, the name and location of the store, and the dates of the sale, if any. A buyer doesn't need much more information to make a decision. Most pertinent questions are answered. If one is shopping for a sofa in this price range, then a visit to the store might be scheduled. Other information, such as "Hot Buy!" or "Going Out of Business," is superfluous.

Consider an ad for a job. Usually it will give the name of the position, a description of the requirements and possibly the name of the company and the salary. If one has the required skills, one might apply. Other information, such as "industry leader" or "dream career," is unnecessary.

In both cases the ads usually supply the relevant information a consumer needs to make a decision. Companies do not like to waste money on ad copy that does not accomplish a specific goal.

Now consider an ad for a house selected at random from a newspaper:

> Roland Hills, reduced for quick sale, 4 bed, 2 ba, den, pool.
> Parklike yard. Broker (xxx) yyy-zzzz

What is stated in the ad is probably true. Perhaps the price has been reduced. Perhaps the home was *overpriced*. Perhaps it was reduced for a quick sale because the broker wants a quick sale, as most brokers do...

The important point is that the house ad gives much less information to make a decision in the same way that a person makes a decision about the other products--the sofa or the job. The house ad has no price, no square footage, no bedroom sizes, no floorplan... For this reason, the ad, while well-intentioned, is a "blind" ad. A blind person would not want this particular home based upon such dismal information...

Consequently, most real estate agents do not take advertising--including their own--too seriously. Most real estate ads are simply throwing a hook and line into the "ocean": the ads offer nothing more than "bait."

If a person calls on the above home, what information, without even mentioning a word, is communicated to the agent who answers the call? That one is shopping for this particular home? That one can afford it? That it is in one's price range? That one wants a home in this specific area? That it is just the right size and layout for one's family?

None of this is immediately communicated--excepting that the caller is a semi-serious buyer. Most people who call on an ad which has insufficient information to make a decision are:

        a)   in the market, shopping;

        b)   capable of being sold a similar product.

In other words, without uttering a sound a respondent reveals that the waters are full of live and kicking sea creatures. And most of them need guidance. That is the role of the agent. That is also why more time will be spent by an agent trying to recruit a caller as a client--than in giving the caller information about the home.

The ad is placed to pickup buyers. Generic buyers--not buyers for a particular property.

The seller, however, thinks that the home is being marketed well. Sellers become "all smiles" when they see their homes in print. Many rub their hands, thinking "It's only just a matter of time..."

When a person reads through a Sunday supplement published by a newspaper that is full of one-page ads for *several dozen* homes listed with a company, most of the ads resemble the ad above. For example:

TOO PERFECT! $325,000 Syl., 4br, 3.5 ba, RA zone,
1/2 acre, fam rm form dine, spa. Agt (xxx) yyy-zzzz

This ad, also selected at random, is slightly more informative than the other. But similarly, a person does not have much data to make any type of decision about the home. It is a "teaser" ad.

When a company packages a page of these ads along with a few photos, the intention is to promote the company. The ad keeps the company in the public's thoughts. And if one likes a photo or is tricked by some printed information, the agent who answers the call will begin a pitch for his or her services and for the company.

When a fellow agent calls, the caller identifies one's self as an agent by saying "broker call." The sales pitch never begins. The fellow agent obtains pure information.

There is no more truth in real estate advertising than what you have learned here.

THE MYTH OF THE *MEGA-AGENT*

A name everyone knows. Nationally recognized. His name appeared in the Wall Street Journal. And He's available now to come down from His Mountain to talk about Himself and to list your home. Or maybe He's busy and He'll send a representative. With an autographed photo, of course...

How many homes can a top-notch salesperson attempt to market *effectively* at any one time? Three? Five? Eight? Ten? Twenty? The answer is "not very many."

In fact, without a full-time assistant, surveyed salespeople expressed that they feel extremely hard-pressed to juggle more than ten homes. Many of them with these workloads indicated that each night they pray that at least three or four homes would immediately close escrow just to reduce the stress. Unless the homes were located in a ghost town, sales agents indicated that with more than seven homes there is scarcely time to provide high-quality personal service or to prospect for new business--making contacts, spreading one's name around... And--the homes get confusing: "Did Mrs. Johnson live in the English Tudor on Beth Street, or in the Spanish home on Willoughby? Or was the English Tudor on Willoughby...?"

The best agents you'll meet--in terms of personal service, communication, feedback, etc.--usually prefer to handle only about six listings at one time. Otherwise, they feel that service declines. They don't meet or help any buyers. They don't take time to sow the seeds for tomorrow.

Yet there are a lot of innocent people who believe that a Mega-Agent is God's gift to real estate. That there is a better chance of selling a home with someone like "Dyno-Mike" than with Joe Simple of Simple Realty. How does "Dyno-Mike" do it, one may ask?

Let's suppose that "Dyno-Mike" personally has 120 listings. Let's suppose that he has ten helpers, each handling 12 homes. Will these helpers be busy?

"Dyno-Mike" is out of the office drumming up new business, representing the firm, attending functions, spreading the word. If one contacts the company to obtain information on the status of a home, will "Dyno-Mike"--the top of the pyramid--be available? Will one of the assistants be available? Will one of the assistants be ready to answer specific questions regarding a home? Will an assistant of the assistant be available, and have the answers?

Some innocent people list their homes with "Dyno-Mike" because he has name recognition. As a good salesman, he tells them that he contacts more people than Joe Simple, and therefore "spreads the word" to more people about one particular house. In actual fact, more people are apt to contact "Dyno-Mike." Therefore, he can easily refer them to one particular house. Someone like Yokel A is excited! Yokel A hears this and he knows that he has the right agent!

Let's suppose that "Dyno-Mike" is sitting in his office (a rare event) and a call comes in from another agent who is looking for a specific house. "Dyno-Mike" looks at his billboard and sees that Yokel A's house is available, and suggests it to the agent.

Now suppose that several hours pass and "Dyno-Mike" is at a public function. He meets another agent, and she asks him if he has a home to fit her client's needs--the same type of home as Yokel A's.

Here's the kicker. Out of 120 homes, will "Dyno-Mike" remember Yokel A's house? Can he describe it? How many Yokel A homes does "Dyno-Mike" have? When those calls come in--does "Dyno-Mike" recommend only Yokel A's house? Does he care whether Yokel A's house sells over Yokel B's--that the important thing is to keep sales going in order to stay on top of the pyramid?

There are many "Dyno-Mikes" in this world. And most of them are very fine sales agents.

But unfortunately, when an agent has many similar homes that can be trade-offs for one another, the agent does not have incentive to favor the sale of one over the other, unless one is priced higher... The agent will be more concerned that the average number of sales stays high in order to remain on top of the pyramid. And the more listings an agent has, the higher the probability that the agent has similar homes.

Let's ask another question...

Suppose in one year, "Dyno-Mike" and his staff list a total of 600 homes. They sell 120 of them. That's one-fifth, or 20%.

Suppose that Slow Joe Simple only likes to list six homes at one time. When anyone calls Slow Joe, he rattles-off information about his listings from the top of his head. He knows these six homes thoroughly, along with all of the competitors, and constantly updates his information against any homes that come on the market. And 24 hours a day--every day--Slow Joe thinks about nothing but selling these six homes. Anytime he gets within earshot of an agent or a potential buyer, Slow Joe pitches only these homes.

Slow Joe relies on six homes to sell--not 120--in order to make his living and to support his family. He has more incentive than "Dyno-Mike" to sell these six homes. Why?

"Dyno-Mike" has *20* stacks of six homes. Slow Joe only has *one* stack. Which stack does "Dyno-Mike" prefer to sell...?

"Dyno-Mike's" assistants each have *two* stacks of six homes. Which stack would they prefer to sell?

And suppose Slow Joe only lists a total of 30 homes in one year--selling 20 of them. That's two out of three or 66%.

The pyramid sold one out of five or 20%.

With whom would you prefer to list your home?

Next time a Mega-Agent comes knocking on your door, remember that the probability of a sale by a pyramid of agents may be much less than through the efforts of one lone hard-working individual.

MYTH #11a: YOUR BROKER IS WORKING FOR YOU

Why do people choose to work in real estate?

Below are the most frequent answers agents selected in surveys:

"I like the flexibility."

"I like the independence. I can work when and where I want."

"I like the money."

"I like working with people."

"I can do what I want. I call my own shots."

"I can work part-time."

"I'm my own boss."

Real estate is considered one of the last frontiers by many in the industry. The most prevalent attitude is: "I work for myself."

"So," one may ask, "what about the contract that I have with an agent to sell my house? Or what about the agreement that I have with an agent to find me a house?" In both cases, the agent is a *representative*. A representative does not necessarily believe that he or she works *for* someone.

Ninety-nine out of one-hundred times you will probably deal with a sales agent and not the actual broker. The broker will normally be out promoting the company and will not have time to attend to your transaction personally. The sales agent technically works under the guidance of the broker. The agent is not the broker's employee. The agent is an *independent-contractor*.

The broker does not work for anyone. The broker is an *independent business-person*.

The "self-employed" attitude has its consequences.

Let's look at one ramification.

Suppose you are dealing with Alice Rep, a sales rep from multi-billion dollar XYZ Corporation. What would happen if Alice tells you that she is in business for herself?

Either she'll get fired or you will probably not want to do business with her, thinking that she is a little "cracked."

Most sales reps in XYZ Corp. *know* whom they work for--the boss, the boss's boss...all the way up the corporate ladder. And when a sales rep makes a sales call, the rep knows that he or she is part of the company, a member of a huge organizational team. No matter how much of an independent-thinking "gunslinger" the rep may be--the rep knows that what is good for the company is good for the rep. And the rep will tell you this.

When you negotiate a deal with this sales rep, if something is bad for the company it will become bad for the rep. The boss's boss will make sure of this.

To an extent this also happens in real estate. Complaints can be filed, public opinion can sour, licenses can be revoked...

Unfortunately, as shown in other parts of this book, the industry has a very poor record when it comes to self-policing. The controls to regulate behavior do not favor the complainant.

The main point is this: could there be a potential conflict of interest between an agent and a client?

MYTH #11b: THE OTHER BROKER IS WORKING
FOR THE OTHER PARTY

To repeat Myth #11a: agents *represent* clients, they do not work for them.

This predicament holds true for the party on the other side of the transaction. One agent is usually dealing with another agent who works under the guidance of a broker.

"Employees" are dealing with "employees," feeling that they work for themselves.

Brokers know that brokers work for themselves, although they often feel like they work for the sales agents... That is another story...

If the other broker has 300 current listings in the office, the broker would prefer that your deal closes escrow. But it is not too important. It is more important that a sufficient number of those deals close escrow in order to pay expenses and to provide personal income to the broker. If your deal is one which closes escrow, then that is one more for the quota. But it is not critical.

The other party's agent has fewer total listings and a smaller quota than the broker. What matters most is not that all listings close escrow--it is given that not all will. It is paramount that the quota or average number remains high.

And what is the best way to keep this quota high?

Is it looking out for the client's interests or for the agent's?

MYTH #11c: SYNTHESIS OF MYTHS #11a & b

Let's dispense with the philosophical discussion contained in Myths #11a & b.

Let's look at a live example of real estate that transpires 24 hours a day, every day, in the real world. The mechanics of the transaction are the same in nearly every deal you encounter with a real estate agent or broker. And these mechanics indirectly generate a major consumer complaint about the business. For good measure, let's also prove Myths #11a & b mathematically...

Sales Agent A represents a seller. The home is priced right at $500,000. Comparables show that it is a good deal. A very good deal. And the market is "healthy": there are many buyers looking for homes.

Sales Agent B represents a buyer. The buyer likes the house. The buyer has seen similar homes and knows that this is a good deal but, like most people, does not want to pay full price. People like good deals. People who see good deals prefer even better deals. More is preferred to less. It is human nature. So Agent B, representing the buyer, writes an offer for the purchase price of $450,000.

At this point, please select a "team" that you want to be on in this transaction. Whom do you think is going to be the "winner"?

Agent B presents the buyer's offer to the seller and to the seller's agent, Agent A, who scoffs at the offer, saying:

"The house is a good deal--not a steal!"

The agents shout at each other. No fine lines here...

"The house was priced right to begin with," hollers Agent A. "It's a great deal! You can't find a better house for the money!!!"

"Yes," Agent B retorts, "it is a good deal. But my buyer does not want to pay that much! My buyer's qualified--the money is good and my buyer wants the house. This is a ready, willing and able buyer--not someone who sees the advertised price of the home in the newspaper but who cannot afford it. Do we have a deal?"

"Go back to real estate school!" Agent A shouts.

Timeout. How is your team doing? Don't switch sides--the negotiations aren't over...

Whose side is each agent on? We know which party each agent *represents*. But for whom does each agent have the most incentive to strike a deal? Could this be the key for whom each agent is secretly working?

Let's look at the numbers.

Assume that the commission rate is 6%, paid out of the seller's proceeds. Assume that each agent get's half, or 3%, and must give half again to the broker. Each agent therefore nets 1 1/2% of the gross selling price. In the real world the mechanics are slightly different, but the distribution is fairly standard with respect to the proceeds.

What if the home sells at full price for $500,000? The proceeds to each agent would be 1 1/2% or $7,500. What if the home sells for $450,000? The proceeds to each agent would be 1 1/2% or $6,750. It seems like the agents have incentive to work for the seller. They can make an additional $750 by meeting the seller's price.

But let's ask another question.

What happens if the deal does not go through? How much will each agent make? 1 1/2% of nothing is $0. What carries more incentive--earning somewhere between $6,750 - $7,500--or earning nothing?

Do the agents have more incentive to work for the buyer than for the seller?

Don't switch teams: you already decided...

Back to the real world...

The seller's agent goes to the seller to "pound" on him, saying things such as:

"They're trying to steal this house. We ("I") have it priced well. It's a good deal. We don't have to let them steal it... But...they are qualified. It is a good starting point. They can afford to buy the house. And, who knows, if we wait we might get full price, or we might not.... The buyer is a "bird in the hand." And they are serious about the house; they do like it. Otherwise, they wouldn't have put in the offer. It's up to you. If we wait, I can't guarantee that we'll get full price."

"What would you recommend?" the seller asks, sheepishly.

On the other side of town, the buyer's agent returns to the buyer to "pound" on him. The agent says things such as:

"Those S.O.Bs. That other agent is a jerk! He should retire!!! I told them that the house was overpriced! It's not perfect, just a really good deal. What an excuse for an agent! It is a beautiful home, though... And at $500,000 it's not bad. In my opinion, we tried $450,000... we gave it our best shot... but $450,000 is too low for this home. Why, someone would come by and snap up this house in a second for that price. If you really want the home, you're going to have to come up in price."

"What would you recommend?" the buyer asks, sheepishly.

Timeout. How's your team doing?

Forget the "score" for a moment. Let's suppose that the buyer and seller decide to play hardball. They will try to come to terms, but both want to feel like they are getting the best in the deal. The seller has his number of $500,000, the buyer has his number of $450,000. Back to the action...

"Well," the buyer's agent continues, "I recommend $480,000. I think that it would be a fair price. You're meeting somewhere above the middle, and it shows good faith. They don't expect full price for the home anyway. It depends on how much you want the house. It's up to you."

On the other side of town...

"Well," the seller's agent continues, "I recommend meeting somewhere in the middle--say around $470,000 - $480,000. We don't want to turn the buyer off. After all, he is in the market for a home and if he doesn't buy this one--he'll just go and buy somewhere else. But it's up to you. I think that we should counteroffer with around..."

The seller hears a number. The seller balks, not wanting to part with $20,000 - $30,000. The agent had led him to believe that he could get every penny of that $500,000, and the seller was already visualizing spending the money.

The seller says that he will counteroffer if he can cut commissions down from 6% to 5%, reasoning that he will be above the half-way mark and will be getting the better part of the deal.

On the other side of town, the speech continues...

"I think," says the buyer's agent, "that if they counteroffer with $480,000, that you should accept it. You'll be getting a good deal. It's a good house, and you'll be happy in it."

The buyer says that he will accept a counteroffer of $480,000, if it comes, but only if he can get a $2,500 kickback from the commission that his agent will be receiving. The buyer reasons that then he will feel like he is meeting the seller somewhere below the middle--not going up to the inflated price of $480,000--which somehow seems like it "gives-in" to the seller.

How far do you think the buyer and seller are going to get with these routines?

Now you are getting close to learning for whom the agents are *really* working. Where is the incentive? Let's look at the numbers.

From the seller's viewpoint, a 1% reduction in the commission at a selling price of $480,000 is $4,800 dollars. Each agent would lose 1/4 of this, or $1,200. The agents know that if the deal were put together, each would earn between $6,750 and $7,500. But now the commission would be cut by $1,200, or 16-18%. Each agent also knows that the seller is *only* losing $20,000 or 4% off the asking price.

How far do you think the seller will get with this argument?

From the buyer's viewpoint, the kickback will come directly from the buyer's agent. If the buyer's agent goes back to his broker and tells him what the buyer wants, asking the broker to absorb some of the loss, the broker will probably growl, "Go dump this deal! Find the buyer another house!!!" The buyer's agent, who was also expecting $6,750 to $7,500, will now lose $2,500, or 33-37%.

How far do you think the buyer will get with this argument?

Better to find another house...

At this stage of the negotiations, each agent is armed and dangerous. Each knows that both parties want a deal.

How do they know?

The buyer's agent knows that his buyer put in a starting offer, and has already talked himself up to a final purchase price of $480,000 less $2,500, or $477,500. The buyer's agent also knows that the seller wants a deal because the agent was not thrown out on his ear when the lowball offer was presented. It was rejected, but the parties (i.e., the *agents*) agreed to continue doing business.

Similarly, the seller's agent knows that the seller already talked himself down to $484,800, or $480,000 plus a 1% or $4,800 kickback. And he knows that the buyer's agent will attempt to assemble another offer from the buyer, who has expressed a willingness to buy through a lowball offer. And so now each agent starts to squawk.

The agents tell their respective buyer and seller that the commission cannot be cut. It would require the agent to obtain "the boss's" approval. It would require approval of the other agent's broker. The other agent would not like to change the commission: it would be less incentive to sell the house. The buyer's agent will take the buyer to find another house. Etc., etc...

We heard what one broker replied.

On the other hand, the broker cares more about meeting a monthly sales quota than about earning or losing a few dollars less on one small deal. But then again, the broker does not want a reputation in the office of being a pushover, or of the firm being a discount house. It's a full-service brokerage company-- not some cut-rate operation. People don't work for free, do they?

But let's suppose that the home finally sells for $475,000. Who gets the best end of the deal?

Let's look at the incentives, shown on the following page:

	WANTS	GETS	GAIN (LOSS)
Seller	A sale for $500,000	A sale for $475,000	($25,000)
Buyer	A buy for $450,000	A buy for $475,000	($25,000 over budget)
Seller's Agent	A sale	A sale	$7,125
Buyer's Agent	A sale	A sale	$7,125

From the incentives, you can see why the vast majority of real estate agents, after years in the business, still feel like they work for themselves...

They usually get the best end of the deal in any transaction.

MYTH OF THE *MEGA-FIRM*

Company A and Company B. "A" as in "Average." "B" as in "Bigger. Better. Bolder." Company A has 40 agents. Company B has nearly 400. Company A has two offices. Company B has 17. Company A has one office close to your home, the other is across town. Company B's offices are scattered about town.

Situation #1: you want to sell a home.

Case example 1207: Steve S. wanted to sell his home.

An agent from Company A came over to Steve's house. She promised to advertise, place the home in the multiple listing service, have open houses for brokers and for the public, network with all the agents, and work her tail off. Steve was impressed. He said he'd think about it and get back to her.

An agent from Company B came over to Steve's house. She promised to advertise, place the home in the multiple listing service, have open houses for brokers and the public, network with all the agents, and work her tail off. Steve was impressed.

She also told Steve that her agency was the biggest in town. A big agency has "synergy" she said, i.e., more "movers & shakers," better advertising, more overall sales of homes for the year, more networking of agents within the office, and--especially--more agents to come and see Steve's home during the office caravan. The agency really pushes its own listings, she said, and she has fifty--count them--5 - 0--agents in her office. Steve was really impressed. Why, any fool would pick Company B over Company A! And so did Steve...

How many agents showed up to see Steve's home from Company B during the office caravan? Fifteen. That's 1 - 5. Why? Where were the 400? Or the 50? They were working, holding their own open houses. Or their offices were not close to Steve's home, so they did not drive across town just to see it. And then have to drive back to their own offices to see the other 25+ homes on the company's list in two short hours?

Did the other agents later come to see Steve's home? Sure...a few...if they had buyers looking for homes in this particular price range. Of course, these agents also looked at every other available home in the area--regardless of which company was representing the seller--in order to satisfy a specific buyer's needs.

But Steve didn't need to worry: after looking at a dozen similar homes in Steve's neighborhood, all the homes started to look the same. In fact, after looking at 100 homes a week, they usually start to blend together. The only differentiating feature is that one or two may be right for a particular buyer with whom an agent is presently working, and those homes would be annotated for a later showing to the buyer.

From an agent's point of view, who cares which home a buyer buys? Sure, it would be nice if one were purchased from the same agency in which the agent works. Then the broker would give the agent additional commission money as incentive for selling an "in-house" listing. But the agent is not going to stop a buyer from purchasing a home listed with another company! "Gooood heavens!" the agent will fume, "I gotta eat!!!"

So what happened to Steve?

The home did not sell.

When the listing with Company B expired, Steve switched to Company A.

How many agents from Company A came to Steve's house during the office caravan? Eighteen. Two were sick. That was nearly the entire office! Why? Because the broker doesn't sell as many homes during the year as the larger firm, and needs to cover fixed costs (desks, phones, support, etc.) which generally run proportionately higher for a smaller firm. The broker pushes the office listings so that a commission will not be split with another company.

"Yes," you might say, "but a buyer buys what a buyer wants."

Correct. But don't forget: a buyer *sees* what an agent *shows*.

And after two weeks, houses out of sight are out of mind. An agent usually forgets what a home looks like within ten days. And that is especially true in larger companies: there is more to see, and thus more to forget.

In this smaller firm, whenever an agent entered the front door, the agent saw a picture of Steve's house with the broker standing behind it, growling:

"When are we going to sell this darn house?"

Do you think Steve's house was somewhat in the uppermost thoughts of the agents in this office?

Steve's home sold through Company A five weeks after the listing agreement was signed...

Situation #2: you want to buy a house.

Which agent would you prefer to work with, the agent from Company A or the agent from Company B?

After reading the previous example, you probably want the agent from the smaller firm because the agent was more ethical.

But let's switch gears. Suppose you select between two new agents, one from each company, assuming that both are honest. Whom would you prefer?

Who cares?

That's correct! Who cares? The agents don't care which house you buy. Just buy something!

So interview three agents, and select one whom you like, who answers your phone calls, is competent, finds the right product, is easy to deal with...

And remember: when a sales agent espouses the virtues of using a MEGA-FIRM, just lean your head back and know that the agent is blowing in your face the Smoke of Sales...

THE MYTH OF THE GREAT PART-TIME SALES AGENT

Once there was a joke about a part-time doctor:

A man goes to see his doctor...

"Doctor," he says, "I'm worried. I can't walk with as much pizazz as I used to."

The doctor gives his diagnosis: "You have a transmission problem."

"Is it serious?" the man asks.

"Not if you change your fluids regularly..."

Not a good joke. But it illustrates a point.

Here's a better one:

Have you ever had a sales agent come to your home in a T-shirt that says, "I QUIT SMOKING!...Please pass the chocolates..."

What was or would be your impression?

In both cases, the "professionals" don't have the knowledge or the image to serve a client's needs. Their livelihood is more of a hobby than a "true calling."

There is only one avenue toward success in the real estate business: sheer luck and very hard work. And the harder and smarter one works, the luckier one becomes.

In the later chapter "Attributes of *Rainmakers*," you learn those qualities that differentiate the winners from the losers. In the meantime, let's ask a few simple, direct questions.

Buying or selling a home is one of the largest and most important transactions a person makes in a lifetime. Would someone prefer to trust this job to a professional or to a part-timer?

A sales agent is like a doctor on call--24 hours a day--who represents a client or a client's home: to answer questions; to show the home to prospects or inspectors; to handle any financial, structural, pest, building & safety, or other issues that arise; to "spread the word" to as many potential buyers as possible;

to "scour the countryside" in order to find a new or replacement home; and to satisfy the needs of a potential lending institution. And above all else: to take any inquiry or concern from the client before all other tasks.

Can these functions be performed if an agent is preparing for a part in a movie or an opera?

As in music, it is not the number of years that one has spent playing--but the number of hours of proper practice that count.

A true professional will dance circles around any part-timer, having seen countless more situations, helping to protect a client's interests when adverse circumstances arise.

Point to remember: cover your assets with the services of a professional agent.

Let the part-timers sing in the opera...

THE MYTH OF OPEN HOUSES

Have you ever given a party and no one came?

Open houses for the public are like that.

An agent might place an ad in a newspaper with the phrase "Open Sunday 1-4." Then when Sunday rolls around, the agent places signs on every corner in the neighborhood as well as on the front lawn. The broker approves: it's cheap, local advertising for the company name.

Then all the neighbors, kids and dogs come tramping through the home. And all the innocent people who drive by and see the signs and are curious enough to stop by. And maybe, just maybe, someone who saw the ad in the paper which also indicated the price.

But don't count on many from this latter category. And if they do come--those who know the price--don't bet that they can afford it. Most of them have no idea how much house they can buy. They, too, are probably just curiosity seekers.

Now imagine that the open house is "successful." Fifty people show up on Sunday afternoon between the hours of 1-5 p.m. Fifty "friends" from the above paragraph. Can you guess how many of these people are qualified buyers?

"Qualified" means that they not only have the income level to purchase this particular home, but they are looking for this number of bedrooms and bathrooms, location, style, floorplan...

How many do you guess? Please hold that thought...

When any of these fifty people come through the door, an agent usually concentrates on asking the following questions:

"Are you looking for a home? Do you know someone who is?"

"Do you or your friends need to sell a house?"

"If this home does not fit your needs, would you like me to show you some that do?"

Of the fifty people who come through the door, what do you think carries the higher probability:

      a)   A qualified buyer enters;

      b)   Someone enters who can use the agent's services, thus becoming the agent's client.

You get the picture. Fifty curious people.

Any time an agent needs to pickup additional client's--either potential buyers or sellers--the agent simply holds an open house. And unless the home is located next to a funeral parlor, "b" occurs every time.

The probability of the home selling directly or indirectly through the open house is close to zero.

Some party!

LOCATION MYTH 1: HOUSES NOBODY WANTS

Here's a quiz that many people believe can be passed without too much effort. Please select the home below that nobody would want:

a)   A house in the hills overlooking the city;

b)   A house at the beach in a densely-populated region;

c)   A modern three-bedroom, two-bath home in the suburbs;

d)   A house next to a freeway;

e)   A house with a delightful view of a lake;

f)   A two-story home;

g)   A home in a growing, developing area;

h)   A home in a gated community.

Many of the homes offer special features that make them trade-offs for other selections. After evaluating one against another, it becomes a matter of personal preference. After personal preference, reality always sets-in and "choice" is limited by income or "affordability."

Which home do you think a professional real-estate investor would elect to purchase? It's true that you have not been given the answer to the quiz. It's also true that the two questions may be related.

Not enough information to make a decision? Depends on other factors? Or perhaps you don't believe that an investor would want to purchase the home that you selected for the previous answer--a home that "nobody would want"?

The point of this exercise is to stimulate thought, to reveal that the advice to buy a home based on "location-location-location" is an abstract concept that most people believe when an agent sells them on it, but by itself is entirely meaningless.

Please continue reading for the answers...

LOCATION MYTH 2: HOUSES EVERYBODY WANTS

Here's another test that many people believe can be answered without too much difficulty. Please select the home that you think everybody would want:

a)   A house next to a railroad station;

b)   A house in an airplane landing or take-off pattern;

c)   A house next to a gas station;

d)   A house on a lot with bad geology;

e)   A house with functional obsolescence, e.g., one bathroom;

f)   A house with an apartment building behind it that looks down into the backyard;

g)   A house in a good neighborhood;

h)   A house next to a garbage dump.

Are these tests too easy based on simple elimination?

Which home do you think that a professional real-estate investor would elect to purchase?

And is "location" something innate that you carry with you, your "sense of right"?

Or are you having difficulty arriving at answers the pros pick because you lack information?

As we move on to the "answers," please don't forget that somewhere in this world there are sales agents who would gladly sell you any of the above homes...

LOCATION MYTH 3:
WHERE IS "LOCATION-LOCATION-LOCATION"?

Let's synthesize Location Myths 1 & 2.

In "Houses Nobody Wants" most people believe that the home next to the freeway is the least desirable on the list.

In "Houses Everybody Wants" most people believe that a home in a good neighborhood is the most desirable on the list. Yet here is a simple fact: there are homes in both quizzes that are perceived as "undesirable"--and in the real world people are living in most of them.

A professional real estate investor knows that all of the "undesirable" homes mentioned happen to be those that are the most affordable. They are priced lower because of their "undesirable" characteristics.

For practical purposes, the home next to the freeway seems like it would be "undesirable." It seems like an investor would decline to purchase it. But if a $100,000 home could be purchased for $75,000 and then quickly resold for $90,000--advertised at 10% under market--an investor might jump on this deal. Especially if most entry-level buyers can afford this $90,000 price tag.

Does the concept of "location" have much credibility in this case?

For practical purposes, a home in a good neighborhood seems like it would be "desirable." It seems like one which an investor would purchase. Let's say that the home is located "South of the Boulevard" in a given town. Then, let's suppose that as homes are being built "North of the Boulevard," the new homes are built larger and with more amenities because of the lower cost of land--and to entice buyers to switch to a "less desirable" area. After a short while, it becomes more fashionable to live in the newer, northern part of town.

This example is not theoretical: it is currently occurring in the vicinity where this passage is being written.

The lesson to remember is this: recognize that when any sales agent tries to sell you a home based on "location," that the agent is using the Smoke of Sales. "Location" is an emotional term that, by itself, is meaningless. Investors lose money all the time by betting which location will garner the highest return. More factors must be considered...

THE MYTH OF "DESIRABLE" HOMES

Let's assume that the "location" factor is removed from one of the features that make a home "desirable."

How many of the features below would you choose as being *important* for the *greatest number of buyers* to render a home "desirable"?

1)   Strong curb appeal;

2)   Impressive entry;

3)   Gorgeous kitchen;

4)   All new & quality built;

5)   Updated;

6)   Light and airy;

7)   Big master suite for the owners;

8)   Good or medium bedrooms for the kids;

9)   Good or medium maid's room / extra office;

10) Attached garage and laundry facilities.

Let's assume that you can afford $500,000 for the home above with all 10 features, and are willing to pay this amount only because it has all 10 that you want.   Now let's remove one of those features.   Suppose the house has no maid's room.   Will you still pay $500,000?   If not, then how much is a maid's room worth?

Suppose that $10,000 is deducted from the selling price for the maid's room. Not satisfied?   Make it $15,000. Now suppose that the home is not updated. Let's take off another $25,000. Not satisfied? Then instead of deducting $40,000 for both missing features, let's reduce the selling price to $450,000.

The point of the exercise is that there are usually trade-offs. And usually there is no such thing as a "perfect" home.   Just ask most people who have moved into one two-weeks later.

In the consumer equation reflecting a home-purchase, "desirability" is always less of a factor than the deal that can be made on the home. For most people, "desirable" features are always less important than price.

Usually there is a willing buyer for any home. Equally, there is a willing seller for any home. It just depends on the price.

Which is *more* "desirable"? The above home with 10 features for $500,000, or a similar home with 8 features for $500,000?

Which is *more* "desirable"? The above home with 8 features for $450,000, or the same home with 10 features for $450,000?

Of the four selections, which is <u>most</u> "desirable"? All 10 features for $450,000?

The more that is given for the lesser amount is always the most "desirable" for consumers. Features, floorplans, obsolescence, etc., are all by-products that take a back seat in any transaction.

"Desirable" is a term in the industry synonymous with "how much value (features) for the $$$?"

"FIXERS" & THE MYTH OF "CURB APPEAL"

Most people cannot visualize what a home can become after colors are brightened, landscaping is reworked, floorplans are altered...

And so when most buyers drive up to a home, one of the most important factors in evaluating it is how it looks from the street. If a person wants a southwestern style home and drives up to an English cottage, first impressions are everything...

For this reason, many people tend to curb-appraise a home. If the landscaping is overgrown, they make assumptions about the rest of the house. Could the same amount of growth be in the waterpipes? In the watertank?

Yet in one specific instance--which also attracts the greatest number of potential buyers--a negative curb appeal works to one's advantage. It even gets buyers excited.

Every broker and agent in town would be hard-pressed to think of some home-- including those that are brand new--that does not require repair when it is sold. By definition, any home that is "used" is one that requires "fixing." And any home that requires "fixing" is, in industry parlance, a "fixer"--although most are not marketed this way.

What happens to a bargain-hunting buyer who drives up to see a "fixer"--only to discover that the home has immaculate curb appeal? What is the first reaction? Nervousness: "Must be a disaster inside..." The seasoned pros also get worried: "Fixer? I've been conned by some unscrupulous agent's false advertising...or else it must be a disaster inside..."

But if the home looks like an overgrown dump, this class of buyers gets excited: "Shrubbery and paint! That's easy to fix! I can do that!" They see dollar signs behind the vegetation that can blossom with sweat labor.

Everyone wants a bargain. When the word "fixer" is placed in an ad, many people believe that they can smell a deal. And if the curb appeal of a home is low, many people believe that they can taste easy money.

But here's the catch:

Suppose a house is in immaculate condition. A widow has lived in it for twenty years. It still has the old wallpaper. Vegetation is slightly overgrown.

Otherwise, the home is in great shape.

Which is the better alternative?

1) Have the widow clear the yard, partially re-landscape the front of the house, and let the agent market the home as "gorgeous"-- allowing buyers to find out about the old wallpaper on their own?

2) Simply market the property as a "light fixer" and discount the price?

People who don't want a home that requires some work will bypass this one in a minute--even if it is not marketed as a "fixer."

Some agents take liberties with the word "fixer" and stretch it in an attempt to attract the greatest number of bargain-hunters possible.

Case example 1444: a "fixer" needs foundation work, flooring, wall-supports, drywall, plumbing, electrical, paint, a new kitchen & baths, roof repairs... Such a house is not a "fixer": it's a state-of-emergency...

For these reasons, number 2, above--honest advertising and a perceived bargain--work better every time, attracting the greatest number of buyers, helping an agent to maintain integrity in the eyes of other agents...

CHAPTER 5

THE

GAMES

The victor looked up to Heaven and the angels wept...

- Anonymous

THE "OLD SHOE" TECHNIQUE

When markets are hot, many agents don't like to waste time with buyers who are picky and indecisive, who don't snap-up houses that might not fit their overall needs. "Why fool around?" an agent reasons, seeing friends earning fat, juicy commissions. "Who needs dead weight?" Consequently, some sales agents use what veterans call the "old shoe technique."

Case example 112. Joanie C. wanted to buy a home. Her income level permitted her to purchase a $105,000 house. She worked during the week and could only see homes on the weekend, preferably Sunday afternoons.

Joanie made an appointment with an agent. She told the agent that she was looking for a three-bedroom, two-bath home in a quiet residential neighborhood. She wanted the floorplan to have two bedrooms on one side, and the master suite on the other. She also wanted a big, eat-in kitchen. Since the agent knew her price range, Joanie thought that the "perfect" home would be ready to visit on Sunday...

At the appointed time, Joanie met her agent at the office, climbed into the agent's car, and they sped off. The agent selected three houses to see. The first one on the list, Joanie was told, she may not like. But it was in the price range: it would give the agent a better idea of what Joanie wanted. They parked in front of the first house. The agent was right. For $99,000 one could buy a lot of overgrown shrubs, dark carpeting, leaky plumbing and--hey!--no eat-in kitchen!

"Sorry," replied the agent. "It's in your price range."

After the brief tour and before "sticker shock" set in, the agent touched Joanie's arm and casually mentioned:

"I didn't think you'd like it. You have more class than this. Let's go see the others."

As Joanie climbed into the car, whisking away, she felt relieved, escaping that dark, dreary dungeon.

When the car pulled up to the second house, a greater sense of relief came over Joanie. "This is more like it," she thought, "better neighborhood. The house is cleaner. It shows pride of ownership. It could have more curb appeal, though. Oh well, let's go in..."

The walk-through wasn't bad. The home was clean inside. Used, but clean. The bedrooms weren't too large, but they'd do. Some of the old paint needed retouching, but it could be done. And hey!--the eat-in kitchen was rather small!

"This is definitely a better home," concluded the agent.

"Yes, but it's not quite right," Joanie replied. "If it only had..."

Finally, after much discussion, Joanie asked the price.

"$115,000."

"Gulp!" Joanie noticed a knot in her stomach when she quietly commented, "For this place?"

The agent empathized, "Yeah, well, that's the market. But let's go see the next one. I think you'll like it even more!"

This time as Joanie drove away, relief came in knowing that she was not spending 15% over her maximum budget on something that she really didn't want.

As they drove along, Joanie subtly noticed that the neighborhood was again changing. Wider streets. Bigger trees. More expensive cars. Then she saw it. A for-sale sign. The car pulled into the driveway and--the home looked good! Clean as a whistle!!! Pride of ownership? One could eat off the front steps...

Joanie toured the home, excited. Everything she could ask for! It even had a den! Joanie had only one comment, whispering confidently with gleaming eyes to her agent: "It's purrrrrfect!!!"

Then, momentarily regaining your composure, she asked "How much is it?"

"$129,950."

"Ouch!"

This time the agent also had the next quick response:

"But the seller is willing to carry-back a second trust deed. With your down payment, you could come in at $X, and instead of 25% down, put 10% down for the bank with the balance paying commissions..."

Joanie didn't follow the rest of this. Her mind was not working the deal. She wanted this house, or something like it that was *affordable*.

Then, the agent recited all the reasons to buy:

"If we hurry now, we can get it! An agent in my office said she is bringing in an offer on Tuesday--her clients are out of town this weekend..."

Joanie had all the ammunition. No excuse not to buy! Excepting, of course, that she would be moving into the "poor house" and eating nothing but noodles for a few years while her agent dined on steak.

What happened when Joanie didn't put in an offer? She wanted to think about it? Monday rolled around and she called her agent. No answer. Joanie left two messages, saying that she wanted more information on the house. And, she wanted to see some other homes in her price range.

Joanie wondered why the agent never returned her phone calls.

The first two houses were the bait, and Joanie had plenty of line. If she didn't buy--quickly!--then this underhanded agent moved on to the next set of clients, working the same game. The agent thought that Joanie was worth about as much as an old shoe on the bottom of a lake.

That is why she was discarded like one...

Joanie eventually met an honest agent who showed her *all* the homes in her price range. Joanie purchased one, living comfortably each month without placing undue strain on her pocketbook.

THE "FAB FIVE" TECHNIQUE

This technique is also known in the business by such names as "five aces," "high fives," "five-o," "full house..." It is similar to the "Old Shoe" Technique because it is designed to pique a buyer's curiosity about a particular home, thereby eliciting enough enthusiasm to coax an offer out of the most frugal buyers. It is currently taught by several real estate companies in their sales training programs.

Most agents can show a client five homes in two hours. That equates to an efficient and productive use of an agent's time. The outing is short enough to remain interesting without becoming boring, and long enough to become fully acquainted with a buyer's needs.

Case example 438: Tim W. wanted to buy a home. Tim saw an agent's name advertised on a bus stop, so he called and made an appointment to see some houses. The agent's name was Barbara.

Tim met "Barb" at her office on Saturday afternoon, hopped into her car and set-off on what he hoped would be a rewarding and fulfilling adventure...

The first house Tim visited did more than bark: it bit. He escaped the dark, stuffy confines with a few fleas clinging to him. The agent just wanted to gauge Tim's reaction, to get a vague idea of what he was looking for.

By the way, anytime an agent invites you out just to "go look at a few houses," the first one will never be the one that you want. This custom dates back to an ancient real estate practice from the days of Augustus Caesar...

The second house was a little better, Tim thought. It had a roof, windows, carpets, plumbing... It was nothing to shout about, but it was getting better. It was an average home. Tim sensed that the agent was on the right track. Still, the first two homes were not what he wanted.

The third house was an absolute knockout. It was mint! The best Tim had seen! And it felt like such a perfect home! Tim could not believe that all three of these homes were in the same price range!

The fourth house was just like the second house: average. It had some nice features. "But," Tim told Barbara, "it certainly is not as nice as the last one."

As they drove away, that third home for some reason stuck in Tim's mind...

The fifth house was another dog, similar to the very first. Tim picked up an information sheet, commenting "Hey Barb! They want this much for this dump?" As they later drove away, Tim started thinking a lot about that third house.

He started to panic, wondering "What if someone else buys it? The houses are getting worse! Shouldn't I go back and see it? Is this what the market is like? Wasn't it a good deal! Shouldn't I jump on it? Should I write an offer?"

Tim later recalled that while driving to these last two homes, Barb didn't seem to have them lined-up. In this particular order? No chance. As she drove around, she just happened to remember one nearby the other, and casually picked one out of her book for comparison...

"Oh, by the way," mentioned Barb, "I happened to drive past a house the other day which came on the market recently. Would you mind if we stop and see it, just to get an idea of what it's like? It's in the neighborhood, and it looks like it's in your price range..."

The pricing of homes is a very subjective process. At any one time, there are enough "dogs" on the market to make a similarly-priced, reasonably decent home look like a "great deal." Every agent knows this fact. An agent learns it the first week in the business.

When Barb chooses to show five homes in this order, she is using a very subtle, low-pressure sales technique. The buyer thinks that there are only "dogs" on the market, and that the third house is a fabulous buy. Comparatively speaking, it is a *great* buy.

But there are usually many houses like that third house on the market.

The old aphorism "Let sleeping dogs lie" should be followed in a case like this. A buyer should ask to see more homes like that third house. And possibly another agent...

But that's how Tim happened to see *five* homes in this order. The Fab Five.

Don't you think he'd better jump on that third house...?

PHONE CALLS: WHEN YOU'RE HOT, WHEN YOU'RE NOT

The following situation occurs frequently to people trying to sell homes on their own.

You receive a phone call from an agent. The agent probably saw the ad for your house in the local paper. You return the call but the agent is unavailable. You leave a message. Two days later, the agent still has not returned the call. What does this mean? The agent probably (please choose one answer):

  a) wants to present an offer for your property;
  b) wants to show you a house to buy;
  c) needs you to sign some papers;
  d) wants to list your home for sale;
  e) is making a follow-up call;
  f) phoned you accidentally;
  g) called because your name is on the "Turkey list"
        at the office.

If you choose "g," you're getting warm.

When situations "a" through "c" arise, the agent sticks to you like a bear on honey. You're hot! The only thing sweeter than honey is--money--and you're it! You *never* have to call an agent back. You usually won't have time before the phone rings again.

Situation "e" rarely takes two days to respond. Agents live and die by good communication. Phone calls are normally returned within a day.

Situation "f" does not happen in the business. No one "accidentally" wants something.

Situation "g" is related to the correct answer, "d." Why does it take time to respond? Much FSBO telemarketing is assigned to new agents in an office. And a new agent would prefer to avoid calling you back for awhile. Odds favor that you will not want to list your home for sale. No one likes a cold rejection. After trading phone calls a few times, there is familiarity and safety between you and the agent. Rejection doesn't feel as bad.

So if an agent doesn't call you right away, don't worry. It's not important. This is simply the predominant pattern of communication in the business.

"CAT & MOUSE"

Case example 705: Fred L. was trying to sell his own home.

Good agents make their livings on FSBOs (For Sale By Owners). Like bloodhounds chasing a hare, they read the papers in search of FSBO ads. Why? The owner is pre-qualified to sell, meaning that agents don't have to go door-to-door asking people if they want to sell. All it costs is a phone call to see whether the seller cooperates with brokers. If one does, then the agent completes Phase 1: the foot is in the door.

Phase 2: the Sales Pitch. Fred learned that talk is cheap. Some agents were darlings, sending plants, thanking Fred for taking time to hear a sales presentation, wishing him good luck. But how many followed-up after that? Few. Did they expect the plant to be grown in the garden and named after them? No one knows... After hearing several dozen of these pitches, Fred thought that he had heard it all...

Phase 3. Fred learned that the jaded play this part of the game. As one agent stated, "If you want me as your agent, fine. If you don't--that's OK, too. But as long as you are cooperating with brokers, I'll show your home." Great attitude, Fred thought. The stuff of which winners are made. Then any potential buyer was carted over to Fred's house for a walk-through. Regardless of whether the buyer could only afford the garage. Perhaps the agent thought that this was the best tactic--for the enthusiasm and high adrenaline values, the slack-jawed, wide-eyed gaping stares, the awe, the "incredibleness" of it all, the shrieking "YOUSA!" that thundered through the halls when one buyer mistook the guest bedroom for the master suite...

Fred at least felt enthused. The agent was doing what others didn't--producing bodies instead of just talking. Should have won his confidence. If the agent were showing Fred's house to bonafide buyers, Fred might have gone to Phase 4: giving the agent the listing to increase his market exposure.

A good agent won't care whether a seller does or does not give the agent the listing. Whatever works out best--for the seller.

Nothing personal. The house is just one more available. Show it. Sell it. Keep moving. Keep rolling!

The agent is a winner, remember?

But Fred learned that something always seems to go wrong between Phases 3 and 4.

Another agent who had progressed to Phase 3 had shown Fred's house to a brother-in-law. Now the agent thought that Fred owed him a favor. It's a family thing now, right? Fred's part of "La Familia" now, right?

Fred's gotta nice'a place, an' he needsa protection from da udder brokers, right?

Fred felt cheap, used. He thanked the agent graciously and ceased all communication with this agent.

Fred also kept in contact with some of the better agents, reasoning that when you sell a home, you need as many "friends" in the business as possible.

And sure enough, four months later an agent showed Fred's home to The Buyer instead of showing the home up the block. The house subsequently sold.

Fred also learned to beware of agents who came toting the family album. No joke. Real photos. Photos with the Mayor. Photos with the head of the brokerage. Photos from high school. Photos with the glee club. Photos receiving the "Top Dog" award. Photos with Mom & Dad.

Fred said that the agents should have been selling cameras and film, not houses...

THE AWARDS CEREMONY

"Well shucks, Broker Billy-Bob, I just can't tell you how happy my wife Susie and I are about buying this-here ranch. It was a hard decision for us. We were in love with this one and also with the Circle K ranch. But I guess what put us over the top was the fact that our ranch won the Architectural Reader's Digest Annual Award for Southwestern Ranch-Style Home Designs. And it surrre feels special. Yesireee Billy-Bob!"

The power of an award. It conveys a certain "celebrity status" that distinguishes a home from it's competitors. The added attention attracts agents. For example, even if a house was recently used in the filming of a movie or television show, it is endowed with a special aura. If one has never seen the movie or program, or the house was "featured" for only 11 seconds, the house *was* selected over others. You may hate the house, but one fact is undeniable: the house has gone Hollywood! The home thus attracts more publicity and showings by agents than others. However, what if a house is special--but has no award?

Case example 273: Mr. C owned an authentic, pristine 1929 Spanish estate. It was probably the finest restored example in the area in which he lived. After marketing the home for awhile, Mr. C's agent wondered how to pummel the competition. As quickly as the idea flashed into the agent's mind, the agent dashed to the trophy store and purchased a blue ribbon and large shiny cup inscribed to Mr. C's home, declaring it as this year's grand winner of the Restoration Society of Valley Properties or "RSVP" Award. The agent then had Mr. C display the award in the entry hall on a table with flowers for all to see.

And how was the home marketed? "As the exclusive winner of the RSVP award." What did the agent tell all the other agents in the brokerage firm? "The house won the RSVP award." How did the home appear in the broker's Sunday newspaper advertisements? "As the winner of the RSVP award." What did the agent tell any buyer or agent who called? "The house won the RSVP award." What did the agent tell all of the neighbors and people at the open house? "The house won the RSVP award."

But why did the other agents bring buyers to see the home?

"The house won the RSVP award."

"Ahhhhhh, yes. Billy-Bob. The power of an award..."

HOW AGENTS "BUY" LISTINGS

Let's assume that Bobo Brazo is selling a car. Bobo puts an ad in the paper: "Car. $10,000." Three people come to look at it. One offers $9000. One offers $8500. One jerk offers $7000. Bobo doesn't get mad or commit to selling the car to any of these people. After the last potential buyer leaves, the phone again rings. Another person wants to see the car. Bobo agrees to show it. The buyer likes it. He's enthusiastic. Very enthusiastic. He offers Bobo $12,000. How should Bobo feel? Happy? Ecstatic?

Let's hold that thought and slightly alter the example.

Suppose Bobo wants to sell his home. Let's assume that home prices are appreciating in Bobo's area approximately 5% per year. Bobo interviews three agents. The first wants to list Bobo's home for $90,000. The second wants to list Bobo's home for $95,000. The third wants to list Bobo's home for $100,000. Bobo doesn't commit to any of them.

Then the phone rings. Another agent wants to see it. Bobo shows it. The agent likes it. The agent is enthusiastic. Very enthusiastic. The agent says that home prices are certainly rising in Bobo's area, and that Bobo's home is beautiful. The agent comments on a few facets of the house that seem like they would be "special features" for most buyers, which will make the home worth more. The agent wants to list Bobo's property for $107,500--and promises Bobo this amount--or something close. Bobo says "OK!" and lists his house with this agent.

Let's ask another question. Who suckered whom?

The agent is "buying" Bobo's listing by offering to sell the home for much more than it is worth. The agent knows that the home will not sell for this price, and that the price will later be reduced. Or that a prospective buyer will offer less. But that is not important. The agent can "twist Bobo's arm" to accept something different later. Why? Because Bobo was fooled by flattery and deceit. The agent has appealed to Bobo's sense of greed, and unscrupulously obtained the listing over other honest agents.

If Bobo or anybody else wants to wait long enough for $10,000 cars to sell for $12,000, then no harm has been done.

But don't *you* hold your breath.

"FISHING"

"Fishing" is a method of obtaining a listing that is currently in vogue with many astute agents. It is very similar to the technique of "buying a listing," except that it is designed to protect the agent while appealing to a seller's greed.

The technique of fishing is quite subtle.

Suppose you have a house to sell. You phone Bobbi Broker, who sends over her star, Amy Agent.

Before Amy comes to your home, she studies the homes in your neighborhood, driving up and down the streets, preparing a comparative market analysis. And naturally, she also prepares to give you a big sales pitch about why you should list your home with Bobbi Broker whose firm, she says, is "God's gift to real estate." That is why Bobbi selected Amy to make the presentation.

As Amy studies your home on paper, she has a pretty good idea of what it is worth, so she prepares three pricing scenarios:

1.   Rockbottom - if you want to sell your home today.

2.   Midrange - the true market worth of the home.

3.   Pie-in-the-Sky - the "fishing" price.

After Amy comes to your home and gives you the big buildup on Bobbi Broker Realty, you decide to explore more pertinent topics. The dialogue runs something like this:

"Amy," you ask, "How much do you think my home is worth?"

"Well, that depends. It's a beautiful home. It is one of the better in the neighborhood, a shining example of...and it has tremendous possibilities for anyone who wants to...and it appeals to many buyers looking for..."

"But it really depends on what you want to get out of it. If you absolutely had to sell today, based on what I've seen in the marketplace, I think that you could easily get $375,000 for the home. At that price, it should sell in a day. It's gorgeous and anyone would snap it up immediately!

"But a more realistic price for the home would be $425,000 to $450,000. At that price, it would take the normal amount of time to sell.

"But if you want to go fishing to see how much we can get for it, we can price it at $500,000 and see what happens. We can try it at this price for, say, 30 days. And then if it doesn't sell--we can always lower it.

"So, the decision is up to you. I'll write it up and do it any way you want."

Amy Allstar. Atta-girl, Amy. Greed is good.

This type of pitch appeals to almost any seller. The agent appears as an honest, truthful, flexible, candid, selfless, devoted and straightforward person who is looking out for the seller's best interest. And because it has natural appeal to the most vital part of every seller's concern--i.e., the wallet--this sales pitch naturally wins the heart.

What are the ramifications? Case example 947:

Three agents were competing to obtain a listing from another seller. Agent A priced the home realistically at $695,000. Agent B priced the home realistically at $725,000. Both agents were from highly reputable firms. Both agents were relatively equal in terms of marketing and presentation skills, experience levels, etc. They were both on par with their third competitor.

Agent C used the fishing technique and got the listing. The home came on the market at $895,000.

Then, all the other agents went to see the home, as usual, because they all look at the same inventory. And all the agents cried, "It's overpriced!"

Thirty-days later, the home was marketed as being "drastically reduced" to $750,000. Three offers immediately came in: 1) $710,000; 2) $715,000; 3) $725,000 with some kickbacks (e.g., carpeting changes).

In this case, we can give Agent C credit. The agent served the needs of the seller better than Agent A. On the other hand, Agent B might have saved the seller $5,000 in accrued interest payments if the home had sold 30 days sooner. But, the highest offer may not have been $725,000 through Agent B.

So who is right? Let's look at it from a different angle.

Case example 1152:

Many agents caught wind of this technique and began using it in a large suburb. Suddenly many of the homes appeared to be overpriced, like Amy's example above, rising 25-33% beyond rational expectations, the homes appearing to be priced without rhyme or reason.

Agents do not like to show overpriced homes. They may preview such homes, and may even retain the information sheets on the home, writing in large letters OVERPRICED BY $X. But these sheets will only be saved if the homes are worth remembering. A home must be extra-special if it is overpriced. In other words, it should be *PERFECT AT PRICE $Y* if the home is worth retaining on file. Otherwise, it's just another overpriced joke.

Many, many overpriced homes came on the market thanks to the fishing technique. Consequently, the honest agents who were pricing homes "realistically" for sellers were having an easy time selling such listings. Buyers in "the market" perceived that the "realistically priced" homes were "good deals."

Unfortunately, this is not the end of the story.

When the overpriced homes were later lowered to "realistic" levels, they were considered as being priced "OK." Then they had to sit for their normal period on "the market." Many of them did not sell. Why? Again, they were not *PERFECT AT THE NEW PRICE*. They were not perceived as being *good* deals. Just *normal* deals.

The sellers who had been led down the primrose path by agents such as Amy had high expectations. Pie-in-the-sky never materialized.

What happened when many of the agents like Amy later tried to list homes with people whose listings had expired?

People with expired listings should be easy targets: they obviously want to sell their homes.

No longer!

Agents like Amy had promised to sell the homes for $500,000 in a $425,000 world. And when many homes were on the market for $425,000, the real world was buying these homes for $400,000 *or less*.

Consequently, these sellers became hostile and did not want to talk to anyone who was an agent, be it Amy, Agent A, B or C. No one.

There is indeed more than one moral in this story. The most important is this:

An agent who uses the "fishing" technique is not looking out for a seller's best interests. The agent is simply using a devious technique to lure the gullible into giving the agent some business.

Agents who use this technique usually work on a pyramid scheme, employing several underlings to help handle the many listings that they acquire.

The agent's real intent is to promise anything in order to obtain the listing. The purpose is to obtain as many listings as possible.

Then, when the prices are lowered to their "realistic" levels, the agent has high market share, i.e., many listings. And if only a small percentage of those listings sell, then the agent is doing as well or better than most counterparts in the business. Easy listings. Easy money.

But at whose expense?

IMAGES OF SUCCESS

An agent drives up:

Big, expensive car.

Designer sunglasses.

Designer overcoat.

Gorgeous suit.

Solid gold jewelry.

A watch set with diamonds.

The softest patent leather shoes...

Expecting a sale or an autograph?

Must be doing quite well, right?

There are many "players" in Beverly Hills like this, giving the appearance of wealth while their bankers would say otherwise...

Don't confuse the images with the substance.

Case example 31: an agent did not fit the above mold, but constantly performed in the top 5%. Everything was very middle class, very non-threatening. No flash. No big car. No diamonds. Just genuine, sensitive consideration for clients and a lot of hard work. Earnings went to support the kids, to aging parents, and for retirement.

Every year one simple proof attests to substance: personal production totals. Nothing else.

Don't confuse the glitter with the gold...

"IT'S ALWAYS A GOOD TIME TO ___ (BUY/SELL)"

Yes, it's always a good time to buy or sell real estate. This statement is about as credible as the old logician who professed, "I always lie." Was he truthful?

Sales agents are not economists. Few of them have formal training in the laws of supply and demand. And most do not take time to consider a client's long and short-term investment strategies, and how these strategies influence purchasing and selling decisions.

Most agents do know, however, that if a house is sold in Year 1 for $500,000 with a 6% commission--then the house should sell in Year 2 for $530,000 in order for the seller to recoup commission costs. And if agents can convince enough people to do this, and the market does not collapse, it indeed looks like a good time to buy or sell.

But who is making the money?

Case example 1511: Client A owned a home worth $225,000. Agents tried to convince Client A that the market was hot, that it was a good time to sell. Client A wasn't ready. The market did indeed appreciate. Five years later, Client A's house was worth $400,000. He sold. He paid higher commissions. He shopped around and found another house to buy. The house cost $400,000: it was equivalent to what Client A could have purchased five years earlier for $225,000. Still, he bought it. He liked it. It was something new. The purchase generated higher commissions and higher property taxes.

Then, two years later the market fell out. Client A's home was only worth $300,000. In real dollars, a buyer who wanted to purchase Client A's property seven years earlier for $225,000 could now afford the same property for $300,000 because wages had increased and interest rates had fallen. The home was now more affordable.

Question: when is it a good time to buy or a good time to sell?

It depends on for whom and how a deal matches one's investment strategies.

There is only one truthful statement: it is always a good time to buy and a good time to sell for an *agent*.

"YOU MUST TAKE CONTROL OF YOUR BUYER/SELLER!"

"Control" is one of the most lethal words in the real estate industry. It comes up frequently. Anytime you *give* an agent "control," you know you are in trouble.

This phrase usually arises between two agents on separate sides of a transaction, one representing the buyer, the other representing the seller. It is an indication that agreement between the parties is a galaxy away.

For example, consider a house selling at $500,000. A buyer offers $440,000. The seller counteroffers at $490,000. The seller's agent feels that it is a special property and merits a high price tag. The buyer's agent feels that the home is overpriced. The buyer's agent tells the seller's agent: "You've got to take control of your seller!"

The muscles of Mighty Ego are flexing. Stand back. The room is expanding. Heads are swelling. Temperatures are rising!

Older agents also like to use this tactic to rattle the newer ones.

What do you do if you are the seller's agent? Do you give the other agent control?

A good agent will respond, "I don't need to take control of my seller! My seller can make his or her own decisions!"

But if you hear your agent cave-in, and your agent later tries to put a squeeze on you, the best thing to do is to back-off. Tell the agent that you want time to respond. Twenty-four hours. Alone. Without causing a needless argument, you remain in control.

And you are also aware that you are working with a turkey.

"I JUST DO EVERYTHING I CAN TO HELP MY CLIENTS"

Beware of this type of posturing. Other examples are:

> "I just like to see my clients happy."

> "If it helps you, I'm satisfied."

> "I'll get paid down the road."

Beware the Holy Agent pose--especially if it is done repeatedly from morning 'til night.

It's like a commercial on the radio. But listen to what the agent is really saying:

> "I want you to believe that I am good."

> "I am better than the other agents (more honest/ethical)."

> "I want your business."

> "Put all your faith and trust in me."

Where does it lead?

Case example 259: an agent who used this pose wanted an unemployed, financially strapped homeowner to exchange her house for a condominium. The agent initially promised the homeowner that she would receive approximately one-year's mortgage money in the deal, meaning that she could move from a potential foreclosure into a one-year safety net.

The agent hooked-up the homeowner directly with the condominium owner. The agent said that he just wanted "to help out his ol' clients." If the agent got something out of the deal down the road, that was all right with him, he said. Sound OK?

Never mind the fact that the condominium was a corner unit located on a busy street and would take at minimum two to five years to sell. The condominium was a less-salable, less-marketable asset than what the homeowner already had. Why trade?

Never mind that the condominium had been inflated in price so that the proceeds from the new loan would be the reimbursement to the homeowner: the homeowner was borrowing money from the bank to pay for that "free" year. She could have as easily obtained a home equity loan on her current property.

Never mind that the agent had promised the condominium owner that he had a buyer for the *house*, promising to sell it immediately or even co-purchase it after the exchange. If the agent wanted the home, why didn't he just buy it directly from the homeowner?

Never mind that the agent had arranged for a secret commission to be paid by the condominium owner. In essence, this commission would come out of the inflated loan that would be obtained by the homeowner.

Never mind that when the homeowner began to look at this deal seriously, the numbers kept changing. The "one year's proceeds" dwindled by the amount of the secret commission, loan fees, and any other out-of-pocket expenses that the condominium owner would incur...

Never mind.

Just beware!

There are more "real-a-snakes" than "real-a-saints" in real estate.

The homeowner eventually found employment, retaining the home.

"FLEXIBLE"

The dictionary defines "flexible" as "capable of or responsive to change." When an agent asks you to be "flexible," it rarely works to your benefit.

"Flexible" in the real estate industry means the following:

Sellers:

    a)   The selling price is high for the marketplace;

    b)   The seller is soft on the price;

    c)   The seller may take any offer;

    d)   The seller might take a loss;

    e)   Help!

    f)   Bring an offer. Quick! or

    g)   The seller knows it's overpriced and wants to dump it!!!

Buyers:

    a)   The buyer doesn't care about the termites;

    b)   The buyer doesn't care when the seller vacates;

    c)   The buyer will pay all closing costs;

    d)   The buyer will close whenever the seller wants; or

    e)   The buyer will do anything to get the house.

As you see, "flexibility" is not a position of strength. It is a condition which usually shifts the balance of power in a transaction from a buyer or a seller to an agent. It results in the following game...

Suppose the asking price on a house is $500,000.

As a seller, you are asked to be "flexible." An offer for $460,000 comes in. You are advised to accept it.

Alternatively as a "flexible" buyer who only wanted to spend $450,000, you are advised to put in an offer of $475,000. You might be informed by your agent that it is the best deal that one can find for the money. You must be more "flexible."

And here is the power play. Once you concede, are those commissions flexible?

Don't bank on it.

Working with the seller, an agent might say that he or she is putting together a great deal and is "losing" almost 10% of the commission by advising you to accept it.

Working with the buyer, an agent might say that he or she is putting together a good deal at less than full price and is "losing" money by not being paid a full commission.

In both instances it may not be wise to accept these arguments: it's all part of being "flexible."

Be as flexible as your wallet.

WHO SELLS MOST HOMES?

Let's consider statistics on home sales and how they are used by some underhanded agents.

A recently published survey in one of the largest states in the United States revealed that most homes are sold as follows:

75%	through an agent using an MLS (Multiple Listing Service)
15%	through a "sign call," i.e., the "For Sale" sign
7%	through a newspaper advertisement
3%	through an open house (directly or indirectly)

100%	

Interestingly, these data were tallied when home sales were at their lowest ebb in 50 years, during the middle of a severe recession, and when inventory levels of unsold homes were at an all-time high. Clearly, it was a "buyer's market." Why would most buyers prefer to use agents in such periods and not find the good deals on their own, saving countless thousands of dollars?

Answer: when inventory levels rise and all homes are advertised as "steals" and "the best deal in town," the market information broadcast through these channels is confusing or meaningless to consumers. Buyers turn to professionals to sort the chaff from the wheat.

Yet statistics like the ones above are used by some agents to obtain listings from sellers, using the argument that most homes are sold by real estate agents, as you can clearly see. And indeed, most homes are sold through the multiple listing service, which is accessible only to brokers and agents. So if you want to sell your home, the argument goes, you should list it with a broker who is a member of the MLS.

But the numbers mean that *another* agent using the MLS--not the one who may be trying to sign a seller up for a listing--sold the house...

Anybody can price a home, put it in the MLS, place a sign on the front lawn, hold a few open houses, and have a good probability that the home will sell. A 75% probability. Any agent marketing the home is merely "babysitting" or "housesitting,"--if one relies purely on the above numbers...

Let's consider similar statistics recently published by the National Association. Where do the buyers come from?

50%	-	real estate agents
17%	-	signs
15%	-	newspaper ads
8%	-	friends, relatives
6%	-	know the seller
2%	-	other
1%	-	magazines

99%		(1% difference due to rounding)

Real estate agents sell most homes. Or at least 1 out of every 2. Sign, newspaper and magazine statistics indicate that the agent's firm "pulled" the buyer in. It is important to note that a good agent is a crucial factor in the purchase and the sale of any home. Many agents will produce the above data, and then attempt to "weasel" people into using them as agents because the statistics indicate that it is the right thing to do.

Incorrect.

Most buyers use an agent to find a home for a purchase. How skilled is the agent in meeting these needs?

Most sellers rely on an agent to attract *other agents* who have buyers. How skilled is the agent in meeting these needs?

For these reasons, is it *critical* to find the right agent with the right skills.

On this point, the numbers never lie...

"WE'RE #1!"

This line and its offspring are used so frequently that the topic deserves special attention. Here are more examples:

"Our office is--

"#1 in sales!"

"#1 in advertising!"

"#1 in number of agents!"

"#1 in number of offices!"

"#1 in relocations! We're your relocation specialist!"

"#1 in closings!"

"#1 in listings!"

"#1 in lawsuits!" (Oops!)

"#1 in agent turnover!" (Just kidding...)

You can take satisfaction in knowing one secret when an agent uses these lines: the statements above are usually uttered by the newest or the least productive agents in the office.

Why does a high-producer have to mention such bourgeois?

The high producer *knows* who is making the high totals. And that is why such an agent would much rather boast about who is making the office #1:

"Why waste words on the office? Let's talk about *me*!"

Beware the Smoke of Sales...

THE "GUILT & SHAME" ROUTINE

Here's an excerpt often overheard that should be on Broadway:

"You mean--you drove all this way just for the color television? You mean (looks up at ceiling) you came *here* (points to floor) just (stares at clients and raises voice) to take this television--and (in utter horror mixed with anger) you're not even going to *buy anything*!!! You mean (places nose close to client's face) you're *here* just to (raises voice)--to *take advantage* of these kind people offering this *terrific* deal??? *You mean...*"

Ordinarily this routine plays at timeshares where they give away trinkets to entice people to drive 500 miles (looks like 5 on the map) to hear a presentation. The real gift is often a set of luggage "valued" at $999 that sells for $9 at swapmeets, or tickets to the "next Elvis concert when The King returns." Welcome to high-pressure sales.

If you are not a serious buyer and go to one of these presentations just for a freebie, then you'll earn the $9 luggage and all that goes with it. Prefacing this speech will often be a "testimonial" by the most wonderfully satisfied couple who rave about the benefits of their timeshare, and who also happen to work for the people sponsoring the event...

THE "JUST FOR LUNCH" BUNCH

Perhaps you've seen them. An agent holds an open house for brokers and other agents. Lunch is being served. The house contains a dozen agents, eating, looking about, touring the property, chatting.

Then, a small clique of two or three agents enters and sneaks into the kitchen or dining room. First the new arrivals fill their plates, then their mouths, then their stomachs, then... They don't walk around and look at the house? They just came for the food??? Yes, indeed.

Welcome to the winner's circle, ladies and gentlemen. You can't starve in the real estate business! At least the agent serves a great menu--that's how the clique selected the house. They went through the open house announcement sheets distributed to all the local real estate agencies, annotated those marked "luncheon served," and then chose this home over the others based upon the entre. Better say "Hi" before they go to another home for dessert!

THE "OUR AGENCY" ROUTINE

Here are some "reasons" agents give to list a home with "our" agency:

"Bigger. Better. Bolder. Broader."

"Synergy. More agents. More possibility to sell."

"Our agents sell more homes. We have the highest productivity ratio."

"We're Number One!"

Who isn't "Numero Uno" these days?

The "Our Agency" routine is part of the Smoke of Sales and has no bearing on whether the agency or *the agent* can sell a home.

And sell it while obtaining the utmost for the client.

Case example 77: Mrs. Benson, a widow, wanted to sell her home.

A "kind, understanding, young agent" came to her house and sold her on the virtues of the firm. The firm was the "biggest in town" and had a "fine reputation." It was "Number One." The agent showed her all the graphs to prove it. So, Mrs. Benson listed her home with the "winner"--Company A.

That afternoon, the agent called some friends over at Company B, telling them that his new listing was priced 20% under market. Three of the agents at Company B brought over full-price offers that same evening.

Poor Mrs. Benson... she would have been better off selecting a "loser" firm with an honest agent who garnered 100% of fair market value for the property...

THE "I HAVE A BUYER" ROUTINE

Too many agents spend too much time driving around alone in their automobiles telling people "I have a buyer for your home." This "buyer" may be:

a) a relative;

b) someone who cannot afford the house or who is looking for a different type of home;

c) someone who will be looking for a home in a few months;

d) another agent's client.

If the agent had a bonafide buyer in hand, the agent would:

1) twist the seller's arm for a one-client listing agreement;

2) bring the buyer over quickly;

3) twist the buyer's arm to write the offer *right now*;

4) twist the seller's arm to hear the offer;

5) present the offer *ASAP*!!!

Number five is the key. If an agent has a buyer, nothing will prevent the agent from presenting an offer. That is why an offer almost never comes from a mythical buyer. Rather, the agent is just making conversation, trying to entice a seller's interest.

Case example 133: Jimmy H. was standing in his front yard, watering the lawn. A car pulled up and an agent got out. The agent hollered "I have a buyer for this home!"

Jimmy responded "Really? Dead or alive?"

The agent got back into the car and drove away.

Agents who behave in this manner do not lend credibility to the industry...

CHAPTER 6

THE

"HOUSING MARKET?"

Among economists, the real world is often a special case.

- Horngren's Observation

ANALOGY OF THE "HOUSING MARKET"

Imagine sitting on a sailing vessel out in the ocean, the sun shining warmly upon you, waves rocking gently as a cool breeze blows across your face, the scent of salty air filling your nostrils, and above, somewhere in the distant blue sky you hear the cacophony of seagulls echoing their cries...

Your family is aboard the craft along with all of your possessions. You want to find a safe harbor, resting from your travels. You seek shelter and food.

As you stare into the distance, you vaguely recognize the land's low-lying profile far, far away, and a tinge of excitement stirs within your bones. Suddenly your attention shifts. You sense a cooling trend. The air grows misty. You turn and see a fogbank approaching the land, overtaking your craft. In a few moments, it envelopes you...

You call to your navigator to come up from below. The navigator brings a compass, focusing on the direction for the remainder of the voyage. You continue moving toward the land, the fog thickening.

You now travel blindly, relying upon your navigator while the current carries you to shore. You go below, giving comfort and solace to your family, telling them that you soon expect to land. In your heart, you are unsure where. You feel the hollowness of uncertainty.

Your navigator hears the faint bellowing, the hummmmm, of a foghorn. As you return to the deck, the bellows intensify. The navigator comments on them. You sense the navigator's confidence, knowing that the voyage has been made before.

Then a bell slowly, randomly clangs, the sound of one clang hanging upon the water before the next one sounds. And though you cannot see them, you sense many other boats like yours in the water, occasionally hearing whispers in the distance...

As you drift closer to shore, somewhere a thick broken beam of light flashes like a towering cyclops trying to peer through the haze. As you coast in, you see the light beckoning, circling, revolving, like fire flashing in all directions.

You turn the boat parallel to shore. You travel up the coast, passing several boats which seem rapidly to peak-out from the fog and then slowly glide back in and disappear.

The different boats are large, small, tall, low, fat, narrow...

You continue journeying, passing a few inlets. Boats come out of them, and you continue gliding, sensing that these inlets are full and will not support your needs. In one cove, you coast in and through the fog see that it, too, is inhabited, and you coast out, continuing your excursion.

You do this several times in several inlets...More lighthouses. More bellowing hummmmmms. More fog, thickening in some areas, clearing in others. Your navigator glances up at the fog. You sail on, searching...

Here you rest on the prow of your ship, squarely in the middle of the "housing market"...

It is easy to see whom is the real estate agent in this analogy. The navigator works with the compass, pointing you in the right direction, a direction where you are headed: the current carries you to shore.

The variety of boats are like all of our needs and pocketbooks: some are richer and grander than others, changing the required size and depth of each "cove."

The foghorns, bells and lighthouses are like the advertisers, from classified ads to radio spots, to friends offering advice, to office tips, to multiple listing services...adding to the din, to the distraction... Each inlet must nevertheless be sampled before a meaningful decision can be made.

What is the key element in this analogy? It is the fog. The fog renders knowledge imperfect.

If it were not for the fog, you would not need the services of the navigator. You could sail on your own, freely sampling the "coves," avoiding "navigator" or transaction costs. The navigator simply has made the journey before. You entrust the navigator to direct you while your family rests.

People move in and out of the fog. It seems like it constantly changes. But that is a point of relativity...

As readers, we see that the fog is always there.

For people on the boats, knowledge changes continuously--relative to the position in the fog.

Like the fog, the market information in any housing quest impairs vision because the information is always behind the fact. This imperfect information is not limited to price. It relates to style, floorplan, condition...

If a price of a home is low and someone snaps it up because, perhaps, "the home is a good buy," then a long time passes before the transaction is fully consummated. The transaction has a probability of falling out of escrow. If it falls out and the home re-enters "the market," then "the market" has changed. Prices have moved. The once inexpensive home may now sit idle as trends shift downward.

There is fog in this analogy because there is always fog in the housing market.

And if there were no fog...

       ...then people would find their own coves and would avoid paying transaction costs...

The navigator merely serves as a guide, directing you through the waters, one eye on the compass, one hand on the till'...

IS "THE MARKET" FREE?

Some sects of economic thought contend that this world is full of markets that operate freely and efficiently.

What is a "market"? Is it a willing buyer and a willing seller? Each making an exchange for what one believes is a "fair price," i.e. a price that the "market will bear"? Is the price of a home simply no more, no less, than what a willing buyer pays a willing seller, the theoretical definition of a "market"? Is price something set between the buyer and seller out of their perfect knowledge of all other prices available? For, as the argument goes, a buyer will not pay more for a house than he knows it is worth, and a seller will not sell for less than he knows he can get...?

No one will *buy* for $200 an item selling across the street for $100... And no one will *sell* for $100 an item selling nearby for $200...

These arguments make for fine bedtime reading, but do not usually apply to the real world. Or better--the real estate world.

Enter the agent.

You want to buy a home. Your budget is $500,000. The agent shows you a home that you like for $425,000. The agent also shows you a home that you like for $450,000. The agent knows that you can purchase either one, but not both. If you wanted to buy both, the agent would be happy with the double-commission.

But since people normally purchase one home at a time, the agent has more incentive to sell the higher priced home than the lower priced one.

Consequently, the agent will often withhold information from a client for the agent's benefit.

The agent will first act on what maximizes his or her own interests, and will consider the interests of the represented buyer or seller as secondary.

Whenever there are agents, there is imperfect information, and consequently inefficient markets.

Inefficient markets are not free markets.

Suppose you inherit $25,000. You want to invest in the stock market. You call a stockbroker and ask an agent for advice. What will the agent tell you is a good buy? A stock with a 4% commission or a stock with a 3% commission? Which do you think the agent will recommend as the *better* buy?

Concepts such as supply and demand curves are wonderful when explaining static conditions. They elegantly reveal how prices are equilibrated. But as Einstein noted, there is a fourth dimension in space--one of time. When a time factor is applied to a supply and demand curve, economists fudge with weak explanations. For example, "consumer expectations" is one which attempts to explain behavioral impacts on price that do not follow quantifiable logic, that do not fit neatly into the static supply-demand model.

And when a series of these models are overlaid, as they are in the real world, the concept falls apart. There is not one but a multitude of factors which influence buying and selling decisions, most of which occur without the benefit of perfect information.

Case example 808: John D. was forced to sell his home, pending foreclosure. Mary G. purchased the home at $325,000, thinking that it was a good deal. "It is good to buy distressed property," she reasoned. "That is how many people have made money." She assumed the loan at no cost and quickly requested to refinance at a lower rate with another bank. The new lender came out and appraised the property at $300,000. That was really how much the property was worth. She overpaid. Under the rules of supply and demand, she should have paid no more than $275,000. Or the home should have sat "on the market" like all the other similar homes in inventory that were priced at $300,000.

Mary G. should not have relied on one agent. She should have sought the counsel of several, asking them to estimate the value of the home, and then taken an average price. Or, she should have hired her own independent appraiser.

But why did this transaction occur, as it occurs countless times every day?

Because the agent influenced the decision. He concealed information, and conspired against the buyer, not communicating the actual value of the property. It was in the agent's best interest.

The agent adds a curve to "perfect" information the way gravity adds a curve to light. For this reason, no real estate "market" is "free."

FIRST LAW OF RESIDENTIAL ECONOMICS

Why do people buy homes? For two reasons:

      a)   Place to live;
      b)   Speculation.

In both cases, people seek to optimize their net worth.

There are two types of net worth that one has in a home: real and perceived. Real net worth is defined as:

      Liquidation/Selling Price of a Home

-      <u>Loans, Closing Costs, Taxes, Etc.</u>

=   Real Net Worth

Perceived net worth is defined as:

      "Market Value" of a Home

-      <u>Loans</u>

=   Perceived Net Worth

Remember this rule:

> People in general do not act upon real net worth. *People behave according to perceived net worth.*

If a house increases in value $50,000 in one year, most people do not say "It only went up $32,773 after commissions, closing costs and taxes. Big deal!" Instead, they say "Fifty-thousand? Great! Let's go buy that new..."

Perception, for most people, is reality.

Even many professional investors act primarily on perceived net worth. Any speculative home is obtained using hypothetical information. The investor estimates what one's return will be. Such hoped-for gains are not real: they are *perceived* at the time of the transaction.

A person will buy Home A over Home B if it optimizes perceived net worth. This assumption presumes similar goods. A three-bedroom, two-bath home next to a two-bedroom, one-bath home are not similar goods. And simply deducting the cost for the addition of one more bedroom and bath do not make the homes similarly-priced goods. A similar good would be an equal three-bedroom, two-bath home "up the street," i.e., having the same characteristics and filling the same needs.

Perceived net worth drives the housing industry. People seeking shelter, people building homes, people moving out of apartments into homes, people buying homes on speculation, people selling homes at given prices--most act according to perceived net worth.

Even a property facing foreclosure exemplifies this rule. The price may drop to rock bottom as zero-hour approaches. The seller tries to preserve as much perceived net worth as possible. As the zero-hour nears, the perception of the value of net worth also moves toward zero. The price of the home declines in an attempt to salvage anything above zero, including a credit rating. In actuality, the home could sell for significantly more than any claims against it, with proceeds going to the homeowner.

But reality does not govern behavior...

CASE EXAMPLE 217:
HOW TO SELL A HOME IN ANY "MARKET"

Here's a little multiple-choice quiz. Please choose a, b or c, below:

1. If you are a seller, most buyers are looking for:

    a) A fixer-upper;
    b) A showpiece (move-in condition);
    c) A deal.

2. The easiest home to sell is:

    a) A three-bedroom, two-bath + family room + two-car garage,
         starter home in a great neighborhood;
    b) A dump next to the freeway;
    c) A deal.

3. Most buyers want:

    a) A home that fits their needs;
    b) A house they can grow into;
    c) A deal.

Please hold your answers and let's look at case example 217:

Setting: America was at war in the Middle East. It was winter. Most agents prevented starvation only by attending open houses that served food. Everyone complained that sales were slow. Very slow. Very, very slow. Two identical three-bedroom, two-bath houses on a well-known street in an exclusive neighborhood came out in the multiple listing service almost simultaneously. Each was priced well at $499,000. Neither one sold. Why? Too close to one another? They were priced at "fair-market value."

Enter a *Rainmaker.*

A few doors away, another of these identical houses came out--but at $450,000. What happened? Four immediate multiple offers. The house sold so fast that no one knew what happened. Except for *The Rainmaker*, who priced the house.

Want to take the quiz again?

This phenomenon and successive repercussions are not well explained by economic models, as we shall see. A simple supply and demand curve will not do it. In this case, there was an extreme oversupply of homes on the "market." There was also a supposed shortage of buyers. Agents were walking around with signs saying "Will sell your home for food."

Why did this marketing strategy work so well under such adverse conditions?

"The house simply sold at a price that would clear the market, the intersection of supply & demand," an economist might say.

"Other homes were overpriced; that is why they would not sell.

"Furthermore," the economist might add, "price expectations were at $450,000, not above."

Yes, and now you should believe that this one home makes a market, fitting neatly into the supply/demand model. How useful is this information? How valuable is it to the other 17,000 home sellers besides this one who have homes "on the market" in this suburb? Or better--to the other 3,229 home sellers who have properties for sale in the same price range?

The other two homes were immediately lowered in price. They did not sell. From all practical "laws" of economics, they should have cleared "the market." They did not sell. The other three buyers who made offers on the first home passed on these opportunities. According to the supply-demand model, the homes should have sold. Why didn't they sell?

After the two homes were reduced in price to equal the first home, people _perceived_ that these two homes were now only worth the same as the first. They were not _perceived_ as being _good deals_--the way the home which sold quickly had been considered a _good deal_. Accordingly, the homes were now matched against any other home valued at $450,000.

To repeat the process, one of the two remaining homes would have to be perceived in the same way as the original home was perceived--as a great deal. What would this require? Pricing the home at $400,000? Possibly...

"Great deals" attract the greatest number of buyers.

Here's another example:

Suppose a home in the mountains with a city view is priced at $500,000. Suppose a home down below in the "flats" is also priced at $500,000. Which home will sell first? With only this information, the home in the mountains should sell faster: there are fewer view and waterfront properties in this world. The scarcity factor makes them more desirable.

Now suppose that the home in the mountains is considered to be offered at a "fair" price. And suppose that the home in the "flats" is considered to be a "great deal." Which home should sell first?

No one can be sure with 100% accuracy.

But as any veteran of the residential real estate business knows: the home perceived as a "great deal" will attract showings at a rate of about 100 to 1 over the home in the hills.

And with a higher frequency of showings comes a higher probability of sale...

MARKET STRATIFICATION & IMPACTS

In any given "market," the price ranges of available homes and townhomes can be placed into one of three distinct categories:

1. Starter homes   For "first-time buyers," or the lowest income levels.

2. Trade-up homes   For the majority of people, including anyone not in the other two categories.

3. Luxury homes   The top end of the "market," i.e., the highest priced homes.

Different primary factors drive each segment:

1. Starter homes: Affordability. Wages. Jobs.
    If people have no income, they won't buy --no matter how much the population grows.
    To a lesser extent, the number of people wanting these homes.

2. Trade-up homes: The number of trade-up homes available.
    The turnover rate of starter and trade-up homes impacts this category.

3. Luxury homes: The number of luxury homes available.
    To a much lesser extent, the number of people desiring these homes.

Let's take a look at general trends in real-world scenarios:

a. A new factory is built, giving jobs to blue-collar workers.

       Impact: Workers want starter-homes to live in.
                     Affordable? They buy.
                     Not affordable? They don't buy.
           Trade-up homes: little impact.
           Luxury homes: very little impact.

b.   One person buys a trade-up home.

Impact: The seller becomes a buyer, and buys another
                    trade-up home.
                          The next seller also becomes a buyer--and
                          buys another trade-up home.
                          Cycle repeats until someone disrupts the
                          pattern, e.g., leaves the area.
                    Starter homes: little impact.
                    Luxury homes: very little impact.

c.   A new company opens a branch office in town, supplying
        work for many white-collar workers.

Impact: Starter-homes: minimal.
                    Trade-up homes: cycle from scenario b repeats.
                    Luxury homes: very little impact.

d.   The number of luxury homes in an area decreases.
        The number of buyers for them remains constant.

Impact: Prices of luxury homes increase.
                    Starter homes: no impact.
                    Trade-up homes: little impact.

e.   The number of starter homes in an area decreases.
        The number of buyers for them remains constant.

Impact: Starter home prices increase.
                    Trade-up homes: prices partially increase.
                          If they are affordable to starter-home
                          buyers, then cycle from scenario b repeats.
                    Luxury homes: no impact.

f.   The number of trade-up homes in an area decreases.
        The number of buyers for them remains constant.

Impact: Trade-up home prices increase.
                    Starter homes: prices increase slightly.
                    Luxury homes: prices increase slightly

g. The number of luxury homes in an area increases.
    The number of buyers for them remains constant.

    Impact: Luxury home prices decrease.
                Starter homes: no impact.
                Trade-up homes: little impact.

h. The number of starter homes in an area increases.
    The number of buyers for them remains constant.

    Impact: Starter-home prices decline.
                Trade-up homes: very little downward impact.
                Luxury homes: no impact.

i. The number of trade-up homes in an area increases.
    The number of buyers for them remains constant.

    Impact: Trade-up home prices decline.
                Starter homes: prices stabilize or decline.
                    Starter home buyers try to purchase the
                    low end of the trade-up homes, if affordable.
                Luxury homes: no impact.

j. The general population in an area increases, following normal
    income-level stratification (mostly "middle class").

    Impact: Starter homes: medium impact.
                Trade-up homes: highest impact.
                Luxury homes: lowest impact.

k. A factory closes in town, causing many blue-collar workers
    to lose their jobs.

    Impact: Starter-homes: highest impact. Increase
                    in number of homes available.
                Trade-up homes: little impact.
                Luxury homes: no impact.

HOW TO BEAT "THE MARKET"

From reading about different topics in this chapter, you know that there is no such thing as "the market." Rather, there is a series of "markets" for given homes as delineated in the previous discussion on market stratification.

At any one point in time, there are several dynamic factors that impact residential housing. The only real constant is the segmentation of homes and townhomes into starter, trade-up and luxury categories for general trend analysis in a specific geographic location.

At this writing, the immediate area where this text is being written is in a severe housing slump. The number of trade-up homes available for sale has increased from an average of 5,000 four years ago to over 14,000 today. Result? Severe price declines. The number of luxury homes also increased dramatically during a speculative frenzy. Result? Severe price declines.

A few miles from here, developers are building starter homes that are affordable to the highest number of people in more than 20 years. Result? They are selling like hotcakes.

Where is the market? What is the market?

By the time most people become sufficiently sophisticated to figure "it" out, "the market" has changed.

You must *anticipate* where the market is moving for each market segment: starter, trade-up and luxury homes. How?

The previous reading titled "Market Stratification & Impacts" shows you how to analyze the available homes in your area.

Look at the volume of homes in each market segment. Look at the trends. What is selling? What is not?

What are the expected changes in the area? Factories opening? Factories closing? Jobs declining? People moving into the area? Will the average person have enough money to buy?

After collecting data on the trends, begin your market analysis: look under the appropriate scenario for the related impact upon the different segments. You can see where "the market" is headed.

Case example 3644: an analysis using some recent statistics in a southwestern region:

Trends in this area:

Starter homes:	In the "below $150,000" range Currently available: 736 One year ago: 1,368
Trade-up homes:	In the "$150,000 - $1,000,000" range Currently available: 14,523 One year ago: 9,728
Luxury homes:	Above $1,000,000 Currently available: 2,047 One year ago: 1,755
Population:	Generally increasing
Unemployment:	Rose from 6.1% to 9.4% in 1 year

Forecast in this area:

Starter homes:	Moderately good
Trade-up homes:	Depressed
Luxury homes:	Moderately bad
Real net worth:	Decline
Perceived net worth:	Severe decline

Pricing recommendations:

Starter homes:	Price at or above current competition
Trade-up homes:	Price way below competition
Luxury homes:	Price below competition

Buying recommendations:

Starter homes:	Select next unbuilt area
Trade-up homes:	Don't buy
Luxury homes:	Don't buy

To work this system only requires time and effort...

CHAPTER 7

BUYER

BEWARE

One person's ceiling is another person's floor.

- Anonymous

TIE-UP THE PROPERTY

If you like a property, put in an offer. If you are seriously considering purchasing the property, you can't afford *not* to put in an offer.

Offers today are written with "escape" clauses, i.e., contingencies that permit a buyer to cancel a deal. The time to decide to cancel is *after* the seller has accepted the terms and conditions of the original offer--which can still be negotiated later, e.g., if the house is infested with termites, the plumbing is bad, the roof leaks...

The most important thing to remember is this: if you want a property, tie it up before someone else does. If the property is a good deal, it may not last.

And put the offer in writing. This instills confidence in an agent because it shows that you are serious. Agents work harder for serious buyers. They see enough "fruitcakes" and "poseurs" in a month to last a lifetime.

Here's a story on the benefits of this philosophy--case example 1019:

The "market" was lukewarm: several years of growth had occurred and everyone expected it to continue--but at a slower pace. The month was January. People were still "digesting the holidays," watching the Superbowl, trying not to think about taxes. Who needs to buy a house at a time like this? Then a funny little ad turned up for a home in a posh neighborhood. The house was owned by a doctor who was tired of the property. He wanted $500,000 for a 3500 square foot tenant-occupied home on a 1/2 acre lot that sat sandwiched between two streets.

The tenants had had a lease-purchase option. Their option period to buy the home had expired. Consequently, they forfeited their $25,000 deposit. The doctor's lawyer already had informed the tenants to vacate the premises. Immediately!

The doctor just wanted to dump the property. The tenants had been living there for six months rent-free, and now they admitted defeat. The lawyer scheduled a moving date <u>and</u> a moving van. The good doctor just wanted to go back to his brain surgery and leave operations on wallets to his lawyer. Perhaps he preferred relieving headaches rather than receiving them... 'tis better indeed...

Enter the Number Crunchers. They liked the house. It had potential. It was big. Prices would rise between January and June. The comparables were excellent. It was cheap. The lot could be subdivided and another home built in the backyard on the back street. Then the original home could be sold at the current asking price in the summer, and the lot for the new house would be obtained for free. How long would it take to subdivide? How much capital would be required? Over what period? At what interest rates? What would be the return on investment? The Number Crunchers ran their scenarios. They did everything--except tie up the property.

Enter Smart Money. He offered the Good Doctor $10,000 in option money to buy the $500,000 property.

The tenants had not and may not move on the upcoming date. More potential problems. More headaches. But why not take the money, re-optioning the property? Didn't the doctor pocket that $25,000? Didn't he still have the property? Seemed like a great game. Overall, the doctor was earning more than fair-market rent. And the people who moved into the home were not like normal renters: they felt that they had an equity share and treated the property well. The doctor did not work on brains for nothing. He accepted the option.

What happened to the Number Crunchers?

When the Number Crunchers were ready to make their offer, they were aghast to discover that they had neglected to run one more scenario: they could now purchase the option from Smart Money for $50,000--thus buying the home for $550,000.

Back to the drawing board. The Number Crunchers plugged in the new numbers. They thought about buying the option for $25,000 instead of paying full price. They analyzed the short- and long-term impact of the new price according to their different strategies. As before, they worked quickly and frantically, trying to decide what to do.

Enter the Good Neighbor. The old gentleman who lived next door to the tenants got wind of these shenanigans. He learned that the Good Doctor had given his option to purchase the property to Smart Money. The tenants told him this. He liked the tenants. He also liked the property. It had a big back yard--right next to his...

In fact, if the Good Neighbor bought the Good Doctor's home, he could sell it and keep the back yard. For free. The size of his back yard would then double. On its own street. How much was that worth to the Good Neighbor?

Better yet, the Good Neighbor would not have to look very far to find tenants to live in the house. Good tenants. Fine tenants. People who would take care of the house as though it were their own. People who would offset any negative cash flow while they were buying the property.

The Good Neighbor gave Smart Money $50,000 to go away. He simply took Smart Money's position by buying the option.

The doctor and his lawyer did not need to know about this transaction right away. They would probably feel foolish. The Good Doctor could have made an additional $40,000. But he probably would not have cared too much anyway... He was getting rid of his headache...

But somebody needed to know about this deal. What happened to...?

The Number Crunchers <u>finally</u> decided on the optimal path, writing an offer to purchase the option to buy the property. They were upset when they learned that the Good Neighbor would not sell it to them. They acquired the "down in the mouth blues" and "empty-wallet paranoia." In fact, they felt greener than Christmas trees. But not as green as money. Smart Money netted $40,000 for about a week's worth of work.

This whole event occurred when the average wage earner made $20,000 a year.

After this experience, all the Number Crunchers could think about was, "Two year's salary for a week's worth of work!" Ouch!!! They needed a doctor!

The old adage "snooze, you loose" is probably not popular in tattoo parlors. But the phrase is good to remember when you want to buy real estate. You can always renegotiate prices downward, but renegotiating them upward will cost you money.

So tie-up the property!

THE "BETTER HURRY!" ROUTINE

It is not difficult to exhaust an agent's patience. If you were to drive someone around town for three months, showing every available home in the buyer's price range and not one offer were ever presented, you would probably want to let that buyer ride on the front bumper of your car the next time you scheduled an appointment to see a home...

Or, in another case, a wily old agent might tell a buyer something about a preferred house that goes like this:

> "My broker heard about this deal. He can't believe that they're only asking this much for it. <u>He</u> wants to buy this house!"

Other variations on this routine are:

> "A guy in my office wants to buy this house but doesn't have the money right now..."

> "Two agents in my office are trying to buy this home for themselves. They know what a great deal it is. They're supposed to be putting in an offer tonight. But if we hurry, I think I can see the seller before then..."

> "An agent told me that her buyer wants to buy this house. But she's out of town right now. She said that when her buyer returns, they're going to write-up the offer..."

Whenever you hear these lines, an agent is really saying:

1)   You'd <u>better</u> buy this house. If you don't, then

2)   Find another agent and get out of <u>my</u> hair because

3)   <u>You</u>, as a buyer, are a <u>pain in the a--</u>!

It is one thing to tie up a home that you like before someone else buys it. It is quite another to tie yourself up, succumbing to the Smoke of Sales...

THE "BUY IT & I'LL HELP YOU" ROUTINE

Some people with very bad real-estate experiences jest that the story of Adam & Eve in the Garden of Eden is an allegory, and that the snake in the story represented a "real-a-snake" who ejected Adam & Eve in order to make way for a new railroad... Sometimes a few overzealous agents are like these reptiles. They give the hardworking people in the business a bad reputation, and it's easy for innocent buyers to get bitten by their sales tactics. For example:

"Buy it & I'll move in, split the rent, and help you fix it up!"

"Buy it & I'll give you a $3000 kickback on my commission to help you pay for that new stove and refrigerator." (What about the carpeting, roofing, windows, doors, flooring, foundation...)

"Buy it & <u>we'll</u> have that fence and tree taken care of. They're an eyesore, and should be removed."

"Buy it & I'll get you someone who can install that new A/C system at cost. He's a friend of my brother-in-law's, and he'll do you right."

Buyer beware!

After closing escrow and receiving the commission check, your "buddy-buddy" agent will probably be:

1)   On the shores of Hawaii, tanning;

2)   In Monte Carlo, gambling;

3)   Driving down the road in a new car, impressing clients; or

4)   Just about anywhere--except in touch with you!

There is no ax to grind here. These lines are some of the oldest in the business. There have been too many situations with too many agents who use these unscrupulous tricks. The verbal support of any broker or agent, unless expressly written in the escrow instructions, should never be a factor in any transaction.

It's usually just the Smoke of Sales to get you to buy a home...

VERBAL OFFERS

Most veteran agents hate verbal offers because:

> 1) Verbal offers between agents imply collusion: either party may be breaching the fiduciary responsibility to the client and disclosing confidential information, especially in response to questions such as, "How much do you think the seller will take?"

> 2) Verbal offers signal that a buyer is "fishing" for a number, and will usually continue "fishing" for a better deal, or will write an even lower offer than the seller has communicated.

Tenured agents advise buyers to put offers in writing; if there is no commitment on paper, then it is unlikely that a deal will ever be consummated.

Perhaps one of the better rebuttals to a verbal offer came in case example 410: an agent was "sitting" an open house one Saturday afternoon. The agent was from a third-world country, and was steeped in the art of "tactful negotiation."

A "gentleman" happened to see the "Open House" signs and ventured into the residence. Several people were in the house at the time, and the agent did not notice the man's arrival. It was a beautiful home, and the newcomer fell in love with it. He looked around for help and finally found it.

He asked gruffly, "Are you the agent?"

"Yes," was the calm reply.

"How much is the home?" he demanded. "I want to buy it!"

"$600,000."

"Will they take $450,000 for it? Tell them I'll give them $450,000! I'll give them $450,000 right now!" he hollered.

The agent recognized the accent.

"Listen, friend," he said, replying in his native dialect. "Go back home and save your money 'til you can afford a fine residence like this one."

Verbal offers are only worth the paper they are printed on.

THE "NO-OFFER" OFFER

"Let's write an offer!" chimes an agent.

Suppose you're wishy-washy about buying a particular house. You like it. You don't like it. The kitchen has all the right gadgets. The swimming pool isn't quite the right shape. There's plenty of closet space. The stairwell seems too narrow.

"Why don't we just put in an offer?" pitches the agent. "I can always write-in a contingency so you can back out of the deal."

Is this an exercise in futility? What does this accomplish? Is the agent trying to sell you a house that you don't want? Not exactly...

Imagine if the ancient Greek philosopher Socrates were pitching you for a home. How would he do it? He'd use the Socratic method--which might run something like this:

"Do you like the house?" (Yes) "Can we agree that it is a fine house?" (Yes) "Can we also agree that if the things were fixed that you don't like--that it would be a great house?" (Yes) "Can we agree that it is possible to repair the things that you do not like in this house?" (Yes) "Do you believe that it is possible that the seller might be willing to give you a credit to make these repairs?" (Yes) "And if the seller does this, wouldn't the house be better than others we've seen?" (Yes) "Then, let's write an..."

The technique of getting a buyer to say "yes" shows the agent that the buyer is open and sincere in the pursuit of a common goal.

Similarly, the "no-offer offer" shows an agent that a buyer is open and sincere. By putting in a signed offer, the agent learns that he or she has a "bird in the hand," i.e., someone who has agreed to purchase a home. It shows that the buyer is *committed*. Agents work harder for committed buyers because the work leads to a *commission*.

An offer also allows the agent to begin a serious, fact-finding discussion with the seller's agent. The other agent has more motivation than the seller to put *any* deal together, and this offer will loosen the agent's tongue. Plus, all parties will now learn precisely what the seller wants. So if you are serious about making a purchase, feel that the home will suit your needs, and like your agent, then put in the offer. Just make sure that you can later cancel the deal.

LOWBALL OFFERS - FOR BUYERS

No buyer likes to pay too much for a property. And no seller likes to feel that a property is being given away.

Yet many a buyer puts in a "lowball" offer, hoping that a seller will negotiate on the buyer's turf, bargaining from a position of weakness. After all, why would someone continue to negotiate with a person who makes a ridiculous offer--unless the seller truly wants to get rid of the property?

How low is a "lowball offer?"

Suppose you own a home that you believe is worth one-million dollars. Suppose I make you an offer of $600,000. What would you think of me?

Ordinarily many more problems arise from lowball offers than hurt feelings or negative perceptions, resulting in a weakening of the buyer's--not the seller's-- position.

Suppose you are making the lowball offer and are working with an agent. In all likelihood, the agent has not financially qualified you to see whether you can afford this million-dollar home. The agent is probably sure that you can afford between $800,000 and $900,000, and that you are just interested in seeing how "flexible" the seller is. Still, you write-up an offer for $600,000 on this one-million dollar house.

When the agent presents your offer, here's usually what happens:

"Thank you very much for allowing me to present this offer to you, Mr. Seller, and to your agent, Ms. B. I'm really rather embarrassed to present this offer to you, especially since you have such a beautiful home. My buyer really likes your home, and I told them to write the best offer they could come up with. But, like everyone looking for a good deal in this market, they wanted to start a bit low, and just use this as a base for negotiation. So please don't look upon this as an insult, but let's just consider it a good starting point for a counter-offer. As I said, my buyers really do like your home."

The agent "saves face," putting the onus on the mythical "they," i.e., the buyer! "Saving face" is more important than playing the fool.

Buyers come and go, but agents like to stay in business...

GAMES REAL ESTATE AGENTS PLAY

What happens to your offer? What happens to your "position of strength"?

Interestingly, your position would be stronger by starting with a higher offer, leaving a little room for negotiation.

OK--not all agents are this tactful.

Let's suppose that you are again out shopping for a home. You see one advertised for one-million dollars. You like it. This time your agent tells you that it is way overpriced--by 20%. It should be selling for $800,000. You write the $600,000 offer and your agent presents it. What happens this time?

The agent begins: "My buyer really loves your home. They like it because... They are qualified because... They work at... My buyer wants to purchase the home in order to...

"It really is a beautiful home. Unfortunately, in this marketplace, with everything else that I have shown my buyer, they feel that the home is overpriced..."

"What do you mean it's overpriced?" interrupts the seller's agent. An argument develops. The seller's agent may have overpriced the home, but the agent is not going to "lose face" in front of the seller. The seller's agent will spend the next ten minutes justifying the price, probably knocking so-called "competitive" homes to warrant the high figure. The seller's agent will look like a hero in the seller's eyes.

Or, perhaps the seller is selling the home without a representative. It makes no difference. The seller obtained that one-million dollar price tag from some source, and in the seller's mind it seems reasonable.

Sellers almost always stop listening when intimations are made that the home is priced too high. The first reaction is to defend the selling price, as exorbitant as it may be.

Let's ask again... Where is your position of strength? Where is your real bargaining power?

If you have offended or upset the seller, you have no power.

If you present a "serious" offer, then all sellers will take you seriously. Everyone involved will try to strike a deal.

If you present a "lowball" offer, then most sellers will think that you cannot afford the home--to put it kindly.

For these reasons, the odds favor shunning lowball offers and overpriced homes.

The only exception to this rule is when you know that the property is distressed--and there is much equity in the property to negotiate. But don't offer $400,000 to a seller with a $500,000 first trust deed--unless the seller is a bank about to be liquidated.

There are also rare cases where one member of a divorcing couple accepts 60% of the asking price just to spite the other spouse... Very rare cases...

Be aware of how "lowball offers" may undermine your bargaining position...

IF YOU DON'T KNOW WHAT YOU WANT, AN AGENT WILL TRY TO SELL IT TO YOU

The only real way to protect yourself in a transaction is to be informed.

How informed should you be? Let's examine case example 1419:

A buyer named Steve T. had been responding to ads for houses through the newspaper. He was getting frustrated because every ad that he replied to where a seller was selling the home on his or her own--the seller left out pertinent information over the phone. Such as about the fire station next door... Or the 300 power lines running across the back yard... Or the graveyard across the street... Minor things that sellers tend not to mention...

So Steve T. began calling ads that sounded like they fit the description of the homes he wanted. His frustration mounted. Every brokerage he called put him on hold. Or they switched him to the "new people" who didn't have the information available. Or they asked him to come into the office. Or they wanted his name and phone number, saying that the listing agent would call him back later. Or some "vulture" wanted him to become her client. He received the usual treatment; all he wanted was simply to drive by the home *first*, and then follow-up.

After much of this nonsense, Steve T. capitulated. On one ad that he called upon, he miraculously spoke to the listing agent directly. He obtained the information, thought the home sounded great, and asked to see it. The agent and Steve T. arranged to meet at a restaurant the following Saturday. At the appointed time and after cordial greetings were exchanged, Steve T. sat with the agent at the counter and began telling the agent what he wanted:

"I'm a first-time buyer. My credit history is clean. I have no debts except for a student loan. I'm single. I own my own car and everything else, which isn't much.

"I'm looking for a home that I can fix up. Preferably a three-bedroom, two-bath house with a guest unit for some income potential. I'd like it in a reasonably good neighborhood and close to the freeway so that I can commute downtown to work.

"I don't want a major fixer-upper. Just something that I can restore in my spare time and on weekends.

"I earn $27,500 per year. I calculate that this qualifies me for a first trust deed of no more that $100,000. I have 10% to put down and can cover closing costs.

"I live in an apartment, and can move with 30 days notice.

"Can you help me? Can I answer any questions?"

This speech was only interrupted once when the agent nearly fell off his chair while taking notes. The agent was flabbergasted! In his seventeen years in the business, no buyer had ever walked through the door and given him a request with such precision!

Usually the information must be coaxed out of buyers over a period of days, wasting precious time. Normally, the buyer does not know what he or she wants or can afford. The concepts are fuzzy. Third parties often intervene, such as loan brokers who, with the sales agent, often confuse the issues.

The loan broker wants to maximize the loan fees and commissions. To do this, the broker must maximize the loan amount, which may not be in the best interest of the client. The real estate agent wants to maximize the commission. To do this, the agent must maximize the selling price of the purchased home, which is not in the best interest of the client.

The real estate agent and the loan broker often neglect a buyer's needs. Instead, they often package and sell anything that a buyer wants and can afford--something that seems "realistic." This may be much different than what a buyer needs.

So check your credit, decide what you want, and prepare to deal with lending institutions.

It worked for Steve T.

The agent knew a seller with the right home. Steve T. purchased exactly what he wanted--and more. The home cost $140,000: it was worth $165,000. The seller carried the entire first trust deed at an interest rate 2% below the market rate. It was a fixer with two income units.

Steve T. rented the units to help make his payments, slashing his monthly payment to less than the cost if he would have had only one guest unit. And, he only came up with the same down payment.

The agent worked extra-hard on the deal. Why? Because the buyer made his job easy for him. He knew what he wanted.

And in future years, because Steve T. bought more than he could afford, he benefitted by greater appreciation--approximately $50,000 more over five years because he purchased a larger house with two units instead of one.

What if Steve T. never knew what he wanted?

He probably would have bought what an agent talked him into buying...

WHOSE CLIENT ARE YOU?

Most buyers do not look for homes on their own; they do not have the luxury of taking time off work, tagging along on brokers' caravans, looking at several hundred homes during the week.

And so most people simply tell an agent some parameters, e.g., number of bedrooms, bathrooms, approximate price, etc., and off goes the agent, ferreting-out the gold from the sand, compiling a list of homes to see on a weekend excursion.

Brokers and agents who work with buyers universally complain about a lack of customer loyalty.

After spending hours screening potential homes, no agent likes to drive up to a reasonable selection only to be told by a buyer: "I've already seen that one. What else is on your list?"

To demonstrate the ramifications of this point, let's examine case example 788:

After weeks of hard work, Agent D found the "perfect" house for her buyers. They made an acceptable offer and the home went into escrow. The home inspection passed with no trouble. Funding approval was a bit slow, but the buyers seemed ecstatic; and, the kids even loved the house.

Then all communication ceased between the agent and her buyers. No one knew why. Escrow received a cancellation request letter from the buyers; all parties complied. The buyers disappeared.

A few months later the agent learned that the buyers cancelled escrow in order to purchase a home two blocks away through another agent.

The other agent had been asked his opinion of the home that the buyers were purchasing. He "bad-mouthed" it, recommending another listing nearby. His own listing, not too coincidentally.

The home the buyers finally purchased was lower-priced. It was also inferior in quality. The buyers received less in value than they paid.

The buyers' original agent is still in the business. She is one of the best. She is a *Rainmaker*, closely fitting the description in this book of what to look for in an agent. Any broker would use her services.

Unfortunately, however, she is no longer available to most buyers. After getting burned like this a few times, she only finds homes for a few longstanding clients--not anyone off the street.

And everyone in the business knows that she could find a great deal for any client, handling a transaction with the highest quality service available...

But most people can't use her because of a lack of loyalty and trust on the part of buyers who are easily swayed by the opinions of unethical people.

So if you are working with a winner, if an agent is serving your needs with a high level of competence and efficiency, then stay with that person.

A good agent will do everything possible to meet your needs.

To obtain an agent's loyalty, you must give it in return.

RUSTLIN'

"Rustling" is a term from the Old American West that describes the act of a cowboy stealing another person's cattle or sheep. A rustler connotes an individual of low morals, one who lives outside the law, beyond the boundaries of normal social contracts.

"Rustling" is also occasionally used by old timers to describe the actions of a crude and slimy agent who denigrates the industry by stealing another agent's clients.

Case example 505: Bill & Dolly N. were shopping for a home. Their agent looked high and low. Then one Friday the agent saw a house, called and told them about it, and asked to show it. Bill & Dolly were busy on Saturday, but had time to see it on Sunday. The agent was busy on Sunday, but learned that there was an open house on Sunday afternoon. The agent told them to go see it and to mention the agent's name.

On Sunday Bill & Dolly visited the house. The agent at the home struck up a long conversation. He asked if Bill & Dolly were "working with someone," i.e., using another agent. They replied, "Yes." He asked if they would like to visit some other homes besides this one. *This* is rustling. The agent is attempting to steal Bill & Dolly as clients from the other agent.

Bill & Dolly said they just wanted to see *this* home. The agent showed them the home. They liked it. They wanted to write an offer. The agent pressured Bill & Dolly to write an offer immediately, bluffing: "Two other offers are on the way!" Bill & Dolly mentioned their agent. The agent retorted, "But if you wait, the house will be gone!" And then, for further assurance, he added: "Don't worry. It'll be alright with your agent. I'll take care of her!" They felt totally reassured. They wrote the offer.

When time arrived to pay commissions, the agent at the open house asked for all of the money, arguing that he had "procuring cause," i.e., a) shown Bill & Dolly the home before another agent, and b) consummated the transaction. The agent was correct, although the arbitration committee awarded 10% as a referral fee to the original agent who helped Bill & Dolly.

Rustlers were hung in the Old West. Such agents should be reported to their brokers and avoided. They lack integrity and lower the morale of the industry.

TIPS FOR THE FAINT-HEARTED

What are the safest homes to buy? To answer this question, let's look at the flip-side. What houses should one avoid? Below is a tried-and-true list of such properties along with the reasons that *people and agents tend to shun them*:

Type of Home
/ Reason to Avoid

Corner properties
   While they have better curb appeal than a house between two others, most people do not like traffic noise.

Busy streets or freeways
   Same reason: traffic noise.

Hillside homes
   While they seem romantic, secluded, "woodsy," and often provide views--most people are afraid of potential problems, such as the house sliding down the hill or possible brush fires. More important, most real estate agents will avoid driving and walking up hills if there are easier homes to show.

Next to apartments
   Most people prefer privacy.

In a flight pattern
   Most people hate airplane noise.

Undersized lot
   More is preferred to less. No one likes to be short-changed.

"Eyesore-adjacent"
   For example, a large, open drain ditch next to the driveway. Eyesores are always hard to sell.

Improvements without permits
   Banks will never appraise the improvements at fair market value. A neighbor's home will appreciate much faster. Potential buyers know this, and might be afraid that the improvements are substandard. Will the new wiring burn the house down?

Functionally obsolete

A one-car garage, for example. Unless you plan to spend the money to upgrade, or plan to tear the house down, most people will opt for modern conveniences when you later try to sell.

Single-story homes

Place two homes side-by-side with the same square footage, and a two-story home will sell faster nearly every time. The house looks bigger, and thus impresses more people.

Multi-zoned areas

Better to buy the liquor store or cabaret than the home next to it.

Bad floor plans

If you have to walk through a bathroom to enter the master suite, and there is no way to cure this, then you'd better find another home. Or, if that advertised "third bedroom" is 6 x 8 feet and has no closet...

Structural defects

If doors are not squared, windows are out of plumb, marbles roll across the floor by themselves, and the roof sags, you'd better get out before it falls down.

"Downwind" homes

If a cool breeze wafts across your face from the north when you look at a home in the afternoon, you'd better go back in the evening when the wind changes to verify that a fertilizer plant is not located down south...

Houses with summer streams

If you buy one of these, check to see whether your policy includes National Flood Insurance when winter arrives...

"Bad rep" neighborhoods

Crime-ridden neighborhoods rarely improve, and are usually "red-lined" by financial institutions, making it difficult for future buyers to obtain loans.

Homes close to schools

Most mothers want peace and quiet after they send their children across the street to school. How they dread recess! And the traffic! And the candy-wrappers on the lawn!

All of these homes should seem like good buys. They usually are. Each one is normally discounted to offset the perceived negative features--which future buyers will see.

Most people prefer a home in a "good" neighborhood with gentle, rolling hills on a predominantly flat parcel in the middle of the block. The home should be two-story, modern, updated, structurally sound, and perhaps include income potential, such as a guest unit.

Some agents have other ideas.

A cartoon was published a few years ago in which a real estate agent was showing a husband and wife a tidy little home. The agent showed them where they could put the tennis court. She showed them the ideal spot for the attached garage. She suggested raising the roof and adding a few more bedrooms. And she reminded them what a wonderful investment the home would be in future years, especially in a strong market. As the couple walked away from the home, the husband quipped to his wife: "They weren't joking when the ad called this a *Dream House*."

Problem homes tend to appreciate at a slower rate than their counterparts. Problem homes not only raise "red flags" with future buyers, but agents tend to ignore them, diminishing later exposure to potential buyers.

BEWARE THE LOWEST PRICE

Here's a quiz to test your knowledge of "sales mentality."

Suppose you sell vacuum cleaners for a living. You are paid a flat fee of $10 for every vacuum that you sell in a world where five-cents buys a loaf of bread and ten-cents buys a gallon of gas. Great world...

Now suppose your boss has another model of vacuum that he wants you to sell. "Just like the one you've been selling," he says. And--it's even priced the same as the old one.

Suppose he tells you that he is going to pay you <u>$20</u> per vacuum to move this other line. What is your reaction? Sound tremendous? Would you:

    a)   Put all your efforts into the new product?

    b)   Peddle the new line of vacuums equally as the old, splitting your efforts 50/50?

    c   Avoid the new line until you have thoroughly tested it? There must be something wrong with it?

    d)   Show both to the customer, letting the customer decide?

Made a choice? Good. Now how do you suppose an experienced salesperson would react? Let's put our Supersalesperson's reactions below so that you can compare them to yours. How many of our Supersalesperson's answers do you agree with? If there is a discrepancy, please note it:

    a)   Put all efforts into a new line? *"Yeah! Go for it!"*

    b)   Push the lines 50/50? *"See you later, slow poke!"*

    c)   Avoid the new line? *"Get lost, negative thinker!"*

    d)   Let the customer decide? *"Yeah right--when I can double my commission? What does the customer know, anyway?"*

Do you agree or disagree with these responses? Do they match yours?

Before sharing the consensus from the marketplace, let's talk about an experienced salesperson. He or she usually:

1)   Makes a living selling a product or service;

2)   Relies upon high quality to further a reputation;

3)   Depends on word-of-mouth referrals to build business;

4)   Will not risk sacrificing a) business, b) income, or
        c) reputation on a potentially shoddy product.

Will an experienced salesperson jump on the bandwagon like our "Supersalesperson" and try to sell the entire new line in one day without testing and comparing the product? Why the heavy commission? Why can't the product compete with the old line? Why does it need the extra push to sell-- when comparables sell for the same price but offer less incentive?

So, too, are the lowest-priced "comparable" homes. They either have been discounted because they have bad floor plans, leaky roofs, rusted plumbing, or are sitting on toxic waste...

It's amusing to see a new agent who has prepared a market analysis of homes in an area, only to have a "similar" home later come out for sale for much, much less. The first reaction: panic! Must have done something wrong! The second reaction: "Better not show my clients that one..."

And the agent is right. For this same reason, professional appraisers who account for three comparable homes in their reports almost always select five homes--and then discard the highest and the lowest. You don't need to show them the lowest priced home. They already know why it's cheap.

Have you ever gotten excited while shopping from a newspaper, spotting an item that you knew was "a steal"? You called and inquired about it, learning that the ad was misprinted because only a fool would sell the it that cheaply. Or that the ad was printed correctly because only a fool would pay that much...

Beware the lowest price. Most professional agents ignore the lowest-priced comparable homes when shopping for a client. The homes often bark.

TRUST EVERYBODY - BUT CHECK THE MATH

A popular comedian once joked about the lack of mastery over rudimentary mathematics fostered in the schools:

"I can't believe it!" he exclaimed. "I just read a report today that says 48% of all high school graduating seniors cannot pass a simple math exam. Just imagine--48%! Unbelievable! That's nearly a third!"

And so it goes in real estate. If anyone hands you an estimate of closing costs, monthly payment schedules, etc., you'd better verify the math. Here's the story of one buyer who didn't--case example 932:

After looking some months for a new home for a first-time buyer, an agent finally found a two-bedroom, two-bath condominium in a quiet residential neighborhood. The buyer was a little nervous, which is common for first-time buyers. The buyer had to stretch the budget in order to make the payments: the condo was slightly above his price range.

The agent, however, nudged him a little to make the purchase. She knew that prices were appreciating at about 10% per year, and if the trend continued-- then this would probably be the last opportunity to obtain such a good deal. And the buyer would benefit not only by home ownership, but by the compounded appreciation on the higher-priced dwelling.

Nevertheless, the buyer needed a full estimate to work out his finances. He was operating on a shoe-string and had to make sure that he could cover all costs. He had the down payment, but wasn't sure about the rest.

The agent "ballparked" the figures and gave him the estimate. No problem. He put in an offer. It was accepted. The unit entered escrow. The inspections passed. The loan was approved. Everything looked rosy.

A short while before escrow was scheduled to close, the escrow agent called the buyer and told him how much money to bring with him in the form of a cashier's check when he was scheduled to sign the loan documents and other escrow papers.

The buyer hung up the phone, nervous. He double-checked the estimate, and did not understand why he was being required to cough-up so much additional money. The buyer phoned his agent, and then went to escrow.

After much analysis, the buyer noticed that the final number on the agent's original estimate sheet was not correct; the column had been added incorrectly.

And so the agent coughed-up $1,276.42 because the buyer did not have enough money to close the deal.

"Better some commission than none," reasoned the agent. "And better than losing a client."

The buyer was very fortunate: most agents would have reasoned that the "estimate" was simply an estimate. They are correct.

In this case, however, the agent had a *Rainmaker's* attitude. She later worked with this buyer on several transactions and also received many referrals, more than offsetting her error ten-fold.

All because she looked-out for the best interest of the client...in the long run...

CHECK YOUR CREDIT FIRST

One of saddest moments in any transaction is when a buyer learns that he or she cannot afford to buy the home that has consumed nearly every waking and sleeping thought for many weeks. Consider case example 656:

Ed G. and his new second wife, Alice, were ecstatic about a home. When the wife first saw it, she called it her "dream home." She walked through the house mentally placing the furniture, selecting the bedrooms for the children, for the office, for the maid, for the gym... She even had her decorations and color scheme lined up--all on the first showing! The husband, too, was ecstatic. He loved the many fireplaces and the woodbeamed ceilings.

They wrote an offer. It was accepted. All inspections passed. Their lending agent had pre-qualified them based on their verbal, preliminary information.

The husband and wife were well-to-do, owning their own company. She was a designer and her creations were rapidly enabling the company to gain market share. He served as the chief operating officer, overseeing daily activities.

Everyone on all sides of the transaction was happy. Except the bank. The lending agent who gave them the preliminary green light neglected to run a credit report. The husband's credit came up negative, caused by spending sprees of his former wife.

Banks do not like to see situations where their cohorts are not repaid. Even if it was this gentleman's ex-wife. Lending institutions want to see the following:

1) Strength of the collateral;
2) Ability to pay;
3) Willingness to pay.

The new wife was not pleased. This was not a "starter home." They both had previous homes and children. They looked forward to trading up, to a new beginning together.

The first step in qualifying for a loan is a credit check. If a record is not spotless, it should be cleaned up. Establish a history of being credible and creditworthy. If you cannot improve a credit situation, there should be explanations and justifications for every problem that has occurred. And, a hefty down payment...

THE MOST IMPORTANT THINGS TO KNOW ABOUT LENDING INSTITUTIONS

Unless you can afford to pay all cash for a home or the seller will carry the entire first trust deed, you will probably deal with a lending institution for a loan. But before you shop for a home and for a loan, you should know how a lending institution evaluates you as a potential client. All financial institutions make loans based on risk levels. Risk can be measured by analyzing the following:

> 1)   Strength of the collateral;
> 2)   Ability of the borrower to pay;
> 3)   Willingness of the borrower to pay.

Financial institutions use the following methods that correspond to the above categories, respectively:

> 1)   Loan-to-value (LTV) ratio;
> 2)   Housing debt ratio;
> 3)   Credit history.

Why are risk categories usually ranked in this order of importance?

Let's look at the strength of the collateral. Suppose I own a home that you estimate is worth $1,000,000. I owe $50,000 on the home. The loan-to-value ratio is $50,000/$1,000,000 = 5%:

$$\text{LTV Ratio} = \frac{\underline{\text{Loans}} \text{ on Property}}{\underline{\text{Value}} \text{ of Property}}$$

I want to borrow another $50,000--this time from you in the form of a second trust deed. The new loan-to-value ratio with the additional loan would be $100,000 / $1,000,000 or 10%.

Why is the LTV ratio the most important?

If you make me this loan, do you care whether I am able to pay? Perhaps not. Do you care whether I am willing to pay? Perhaps not.

You might hope that I never pay--because then you can foreclose, take the property, sell it at a discounted price of $800,000, and charge me a lot of fees in the process.

Is your money protected with this low LTV ratio?

Savings & loans, banks and mortgage companies are usually reasonably liberal in appreciating markets, allowing up to 90-95% LTV ratios. If real estate markets are appreciating 10% per year, they will gladly lend you 95% on a home: in two years your home will be worth over 120% of what you paid. They will be protected by the collateral of equity in the home.

Second trust deed lenders are more conservative because the holder of the first trust deed has first right to get paid. Because the holder of the second trust deed must stand in line for the money, the second trust deed lender wants a low LTV ratio to make sure that there is a cushion of collateral in the event that the home is sold.

For example, if this $1,000,000 home had a first trust deed of $50,000 and a second trust deed of $900,000, the LTV ratio would be 95% and the second trust deed holder would bear considerable risk. Especially if the first trust deed holder wanted to sell the property for $800,000. The second trust deed holder would gladly cough-up $50,000 to prevent this from happening.

The second trust deed holder prefers low LTV ratios of around 65-75%, allowing a comfortable margin in the event of default. The higher the credit risk that a borrower appears to be, the lower the lending institutions will want the LTV ratio.

The housing debt ratio quantifies a borrower as a personal credit risk, expressing one's ability to pay.

The housing debt ratio is defined as the percentage of gross monthly income that is consumed by one's housing expense:

Housing   Proposed Monthly Housing Payment

Debt =   divided by

Ratio   Adjusted Gross Monthly Income

Suppose you earn $3500 per month. Suppose that of this amount, $500 goes to pay other outstanding debts--a credit card balance and a car payment. Your adjusted gross income is therefore $3000. Suppose the home you want to buy will cost you $1000 per month including taxes and insurance. Your housing debt ratio is $1000/3000 or 33%. That is about the top rate--33%--that lending institutions want to see. If your housing debt ratio is above this, they usually require a larger down payment in order to decrease the LTV ratio, thereby reducing their risk.

You can easily calculate your adjusted gross income. How do you calculate the proposed monthly housing payment?

As a general rule, use 1% of the loan amount. If you are buying a home for $120,000 and you have $20,000 to put down, you will need a loan of $100,000. The monthly payment on this loan, including taxes and insurance usually runs 1% of the loan amount, or here about $1000 per month.

Using the 33% housing debt ratio rule, this $1000 a month payment should only be about one-third of your adjusted monthly gross income.

The last information--willingness to pay--is evidenced by credit history. It should be spotless. Otherwise, expect to come up with a higher down payment to reduce the LTV ratio.

SHOP FOR 3X YOUR ANNUAL GROSS INCOME

Let's assume that you have good credit, a few minor monthly debt payments, and that you know what type of home you want to buy. As a general rule, in what price range should you be shopping?

As a rule of thumb, you can shop for three-times your annual gross income.

For example, assume that you and/or a spouse earn $100,000 per year. You can shop for a home in the $300,000 price range.

If you earn $100,000 a year, your monthly gross earnings are $8333. Most lending institutions want to see a loan-to-value ratio of no more than 33%, which in this example would equal $2750 per month. This is how much a conservative lender will allow you to pay per month for your housing expense.

The house payment on a $300,000 loan will usually average 1% per month, including principle, interest, taxes, utilities and insurance (or PITUI, for short).

In this case, 1% equals $3000 per month.

You may say "$3000 a month is more that the $2750 the lender will allow."

Correct. But few people pay full price for a home. Even if one does, the lender will probably require 10% down, meaning a loan amount of $300,000 less 10% or $30,000, which equals $270,000. And 1% per month of $270,000 is $2700.

Here's a more accurate example:

Home advertised:	$315,000
Purchase price:	300,000
Down payment of 10%:	30,000
Net loan amount:	270,000
Monthly Principle & Interest @ 9%for 30 yrs	2,156
Average Monthly Taxes @ 1.25%	312
Average Monthly Utilities	150
Average Monthly Insurance	75

Total Monthly Housing Expense	$ 2,693

(Note: each 1% change in the interest rate equals approximately $75 per month per $100,000 of loan outstanding.)

Using the example, this total monthly housing expense equals a housing ratio of 32%.

So take your pick: crank out all the numbers, or remember this simple rule.

And don't forget--you're just shopping!

CHAPTER 8

SELLER

BEWARE

There lives more faith in honest doubt,

believe me, than in half the creeds.

-Tennyson, *In Memoriam*

MAILERS

It is jokingly reported that when Christopher Columbus first landed on the shores of Cuba, he looked down into the sand and found a very old note:

"JUST LISTED! Virgin territory located northward at..."

- Viking Realty -

So, Columbus climbed back aboard his ship and sailed north a few hundred miles.

Then, landing in Florida, he discovered that Viking Realty's listing had expired. He immediately shredded the old Viking sign, staked his claim, and cajoled the owners into giving him a lease-purchase option...

That marks the earliest known American real estate mailer. And most of them are about as truthful as this anecdote.

Another frequent tactic is the "JUST SOLD!" mailer. It is a true testimonial to an agent's and to a firm's effectiveness.

But if you pickup a mailer you will see that it usually contains none of the information that you need to evaluate the agent's ability to meet *your* needs.

How many homes has the agent sold? Over what period? Out of how many? With how much help? How close to the asking price? After how long on the market? How many of them are just like *your* home? How long has the agent been in business? Does the agent have time to meet your needs? Or is the agent too busy, working a "pyramid scheme"? Is the agent an expert in handling your particular concerns? Simple, basic questions.

Mailers are designed only to keep the agent's and the firm's names in your uppermost thoughts.

People usually don't respond to the mailer that is three years old, one year old, or six months old--but--to the most recent in their thoughts. That is all they are for.

COMMISSIONS & SUPER-COMMISSIONS

Commissions are variable figures in the industry, representing an incentive to sell a home. As such, commissions are normally paid out of the seller's proceeds.

Consequently, both agents in a transaction--one representing a buyer, the other representing a seller--have an obligation to obtain the best possible deal for the *seller*. And not too coincidentally, this also means the highest commission amount will be earned by the agents.

People work harder for higher incentives. And if a 6% commission is standard in an area, many agents looking for homes for buyers often ignore the homes offering only 5%.

Regardless of what an agent may say to the contrary, many companies have been known to work for only 3-4% commission or less--especially on large deals for powerful developers or for wealthy clients who generate a lot of business for an agency.

But for the "little person" such influence is rarely held.

The quality of an agent should always be more important than the commission being paid. It is better to pay an extra percentage point for superior service and results than to suffer the indignation, lost time and wasted efforts of an inferior salesperson.

But how much commission is too much...?

Suppose an agent recommends that a home be priced at $X dollars, comparable to other homes. Normal commissions on $X houses are 6%. The agent recommends offering a *10%* commission and a new car to the selling broker. Will it sell faster?

It will attract more sales agents.

What is the first thing that an agent says when he or she enters the home, picks up an information sheet and sees the commission being offered?

"Wow! I'd love to sell <u>this</u> house!!!"

Money is like flypaper.

All of the agents will talk about how they dearly want to sell the home.

But will this gimmick sell it?

Let's ask another question. Suppose you, as a buyer, come to see the home. You like the house. It's like the other comparable homes priced at $X dollars. Your agent is really pointing out the positive features of the home. Sounds like she wants to buy it. No--she wants *you* to buy it! You pick up an information sheet on the house and in the written description see that the home offers a 10% commission and a new car to the successful salesperson. What is your first reaction?

"Why do they need to offer so much of an incentive? What's wrong with it? Is this house a lemon? Are they just desperate? Why not a normal 6% commission?"

These are often the first reactions. You don't need to be mathematically astute to comprehend that the agent pushing the house is also a "lemon." Why? If comparable homes sell at 6%, why can't you, as a buyer, pocket the 10%-6% or 4% difference and drive away in the new car? The agent still makes the same commission as on other normal houses. In whose interest is the agent most concerned...?

Buyers tend to become offended. Smart buyers will shop for another home, and probably another agent. Or, if a seller is lucky, an offer will be presented of:

Asking price

less:	4% (10%-6%)
less:	Cost of the new car
less:	Extras ("House is a lemon" factor)
less:	Extras (Perceived desperation factor)
	--------------------------------------
equals:	Discounted price

If you try this trick, at least you will have room to reduce the asking price-- which you inevitably will. And more agents than usual will see and talk about the home.

But--you will lose valuable selling time in the process.

GIMMICKS: RAFFLES

An agent dreams up the bright idea of holding a raffle for all the other agents who visit a home:

> "Win a trip for two to Hawaii!" (Or, if you are in Hawaii, win a trip for two to Alaska...?)

> "Win a pair of tickets to Le Chaunticlaire French Cuisine Internationale, B.P., followed by a Rachmaninoff concerto at..."

Do these gimmicks pull in sales agents?

Yes, if they have nothing else to do--except come to the home and fill out a raffle ticket. And they'll probably have nothing else to do when they get back to the office. Why should they? They did the afternoon's work filling out the raffle ticket...

Surveys indicate that *top agents* do not like to take productive time away from direct marketing efforts to do something unrelated to selling a home.

Filling out raffle tickets is an item ranked low on the surveys in relation to selling a home.

Top producers who hold such raffles do so because, in one respondent's harsh words, "the cream likes to pull in the fat."

"And the winner is..."

PARASITES & BOILER ROOMS

The following situation frequently occurs to sellers attempting FSBOs (For Sale By Owners). It occasionally happens to sellers who are being represented by an agent or a broker. In either case, let's test your marketing skills.

Situation: you place a "For Sale" sign on your front lawn. Two weeks pass. The only people who come to see your home or express any interest in it are your gardener (who has a cousin who may be interested), your Uncle Willy (who lives across the street), and several real estate agents out "preaching the word," trying to drum-up new business.

Not too thrilled by the results, you decide to place an ad in the local paper, reasoning that there is a higher probability that someone who is looking for a home will open up the advertisements rather than drive down the street and see your sign. It's easier for people to let their fingers do the walking.

The phone starts ringing. Some prospects sound excited and want to see the home. Some sound bad, not liking the price, location...

The ad expires. You wait two-weeks to see if others call. You have someone who is interested and you hope that they are going to write an offer. The paper has been calling you, trying to get you to renew the ad. The prospective deal falls through. It's starting to get lonely again. The job doesn't seem as easy as anticipated.

Then the phone rings. A voice on the other end of the line says something like:

"Hello, Mr./Mrs. _____. I'm Bud Frazier of the Jujube Marketing Group. We represent over one-hundred newspapers in the Near East. We do not work for the papers, but work as a marketing group representing real estate sellers such as yourself. Our largest and most successful marketing campaign appears in the Tibetan Times. Have you heard of the Tibetan Times?"

"No."

"Well, the Tibetan Times has a readership of over ten-million people daily. Many of them are professional investors who buy in your area. We have had great success in selling homes in your area through this type of marketing effort.

"You see, Mr./Mrs. _____, when we run ads marketing your home, the ads are very detailed. The investor knows as much about your home as you do. We include the price, location, number of bedrooms, bathrooms, square footage, lot size, style of the home, any special features and any other information that you feel might be important.

"We publish the information, of course, in Tibetanese so that the greatest number of readers in the country can understand it. Each time the ad is published, you receive a written copy from the newspaper in the native language as proof that your ad ran.

"As you know, Tibet is a very wealthy country. And as you know, many wealthy Tibetans have been moving here recently. Interested people who see our ads frequently relocate to your area or are already doing business there. They often come in person to see the home, or send a relative, since many live in the area already. And when they do come, be prepared to move because they know so much about your home. They have researched it carefully and have limited their choices. They know exactly what they are looking for.

"And usually they pay all cash. Since their country is so much wealthier than ours, they usually bring the money with them to escape currency detection and taxes...

"Because we have been retained by many newspapers, we obtain special rates-- much lower than for standard periodicals in your area. We are running a special right now in order to fill one of the blocks of ad space that we have reserved.

"The ad comes out on a special green supplement--called the "Green Sheet," and is read by all of the people interested in purchasing real estate in the country.

"Now, I recommend that you run your ad for six consecutive Sundays in order to gain the maximum amount of exposure. Or at least four Sundays since repeat advertising is the best. We have found these exposure frequencies to be the most successful.

"The ad rate for six weeks, because of our current special, runs $115. For four weeks, it's $95. As your marketing coordinator, I personally help you write the ad so that it will have all of the details that our buyers are looking for and will receive the greatest amount of exposure.

"As I've said, Mr./Mrs. _____, we have had great success selling homes in your area through this international marketing effort. Are you interested?"

"Well, I..."

"Well, Mr./Mrs. _____, if you would like to wait a few weeks to decide, that is fine, although the ad rates will be slightly higher if you order later. Still, as you probably know, they are much lower than in your area.

"So if you want to think about it, that's fine. I have your number, and I'll call you back..."

Tough decision? Six weeks are certainly cheaper per week than four weeks. And the ad rates are going up...

Let's examine the facts.

It is a real marketing group. Your home really does appear in the described advertisement. You do receive proof--although you don't read the language. And, the ad rates are much lower than for your area. More important, you will be attracting an international audience with your ad--not just the "local yokels" like the guy with the house for sale next door. Talk about competitive? You'll have your own international marketing firm! You'll be one giant step ahead of the competition!

And all cash? Coming to your front door to see your home? Wow! What have you got to lose, except maybe $115 or so... You need to spend money on advertising anyway, right? Why, look how many people your last ad pulled in! And these readers have something different. All of them have money!

...Guess you've already made up your mind... and now you certainly know a lot about this subject...

But let's ask a few questions...

Why do all those people on the other side of the world want to come to your town? If they're so wise, why don't they just order a local paper? Or since their relatives are here, why don't they have *them* do that? Or wait until they visit?

And what are they doing with all that cash? Seems like some important people. Seems like they would be busy. If they are busy, why don't they just enlist the aid of a local agent to find them a house? Why waste a busy person's time on the other side of the world looking for houses that he or she can't see right away? And even if a person could see them, most of those houses would probably be gone by the time he or she got here with that suitcase full of cash...

Real estate markets are local. A house on one street is not the same as a house down the road next to a liquor store--no matter what the ad says. One block may be prosperous, the other may be crime-ridden.

The idea of the ads is not wrong. It's good to promote your area around the world. Especially if your local Chamber of Commerce does it. It's good for ads for "Anytown" to appear in international periodicals which may promote tourism.

Of course, if you were sitting in your armchair reading your local paper and saw a few ads for homes in Tibet at what seemed like ridiculously low prices, you probably would not want to visit, thinking that the people were somewhat poor and desperate--especially if they were going to the Herculean effort of advertising internationally...

Ads like the ones from Jujube Marketing Group can work--sometimes--such as when you are selling villas or islands to people who are wealthy enough not to care about money. You take the chance that they will see the ad in a magazine in a hair salon. In all likelihood, however, they will have one of their representatives handle the assignment of looking for them...

In other variations of this scheme, firms boast about publishing their own periodicals for distribution to wealthy areas or countries. Supposedly, it gives the firm prestige in a seller's eyes.

The journal is usually a monthly publication done in a slick & glossy, full-color format. Houses never looked so good. They make for great reading in hair salons. And they do attract buyers. Photo ads garner more interest than standard print ads.

More important, these journals attract *generic buyers* for the firms. The companies know this. As a reader, you may not be impressed by one or two smashing, monthly, exclusive, color pictorials about the Monteif's home on pages 44-45, but you will be impressed by the entire collection published by State Real Estate, and the State Real Estate Company, "Representing All-State's Estates, and All Estates in the States. So shop with Joe State's, ladies and gentlemen, of Joe States Realty."

You will remember Joe States Realty. Joe States knows this.

When someone travels to the States, who will he or she call to show the homes? Joe Sample of Simple-Sample Realty? Probably not. More than likely it will be Joe States.

For this reason, you should never have to pay for these ads.

Let Joe States of Joe States Estates do it. Let your local Chamber of Commerce run ads in Tibet.

And the National Real Estate Tattler? Or the National Real Estate Exchangor? What do you do when they call you with the same boiler-room type of sales pitch as given above?

Just ask if they can guarantee some showings for your home or your money back. Any local broker or sales agent works like this. You do not pay them to list your home. They work on commission. They recommend prices and market the home in order to get qualified buyers to see it. The more showings, the higher the probability of a sale. No showings: they starve.

"Now can I guarantee a truckload of 30 Tibetans at your home by 6 p.m. this Sunday?

"Why sure... just give me your credit card number and we'll fly your Tibetans in tonight..."

"MAGIC SCENTS" & "BROWN PAPER" TRICKS

Case example 2916: an apartment manager operates a large complex for a well-known, successful, wealthy actor. The rents are higher than average. The building offers no special amenities. The normal vacancy rate in this area is 8-10%. While the building has higher than average "turnover" or people moving out, the manager usually runs the complex at a vacancy rate of 2-3%. None of the new tenants know who owns the building. How does the manager rent the units so quickly?

Have you ever walked into a bathroom after the last person lost a lunch? Do you remember your reaction? Disgusted? Wanted to get out fast? The smell bothered you?

On the other end of the spectrum, have you ever walked into a spotless bathroom that was heavenly scented with jasmine or wild roses? What was your reaction? Perhaps you wanted to linger? You didn't mind slowing the pace? The fragrance brought back pleasant memories of spring or summer...?

Even after prospective tenants look at competing buildings, many return to this complex. The perception is that this building is a better place to live, is "homier" and has more to offer.

How is it done? The manager purchases a scented baking soda, such as a "Jasmine" or "Potpourri" fragrance, and applies it to the carpet. This treatment works better than air fresheners and incense.

Many professional sales agents use a similar trick, purchasing a bottle of pure vanilla extract for an open house. The agents place some of the extract in the oven, turning on the heat. In a few minutes, the house smells like a bakery, and delightful memories return to everyone who enters the door.

People stay longer and express greater appreciation when one uses neutral, aromatic scents. The scents put a smile on peoples' faces when they enter, striking a primal chord without uttering a sound. People feel safer, warmer. And they are eager to express their gratitude. It takes the "edge" off meeting strangers, encouraging friendly communication.

The manager also uses one other gimmick besides "magic scents" to rent the units quickly. It is the "brown paper" trick.

Have you ever gone to an open house in an old, used building that had dirty floors or carpeting? Have you ever gone to an open house in a new housing tract where you could imagine that 5000 camels trekked across the carpet before you arrived? You could see shoe stains in the bathrooms, smudge marks in the kitchen, toe marks on the stairs? What was your reaction? Afraid that the stains would not be removed before you rented or purchased the home?

Have you ever been to a new housing tract where, when you entered the model home, you noticed brown paper on the floor which directed your path from room to room? Did the model home feel clean? Did the carpeting or flooring beyond the brown paper look cleaner than the flooring in the paragraph above? Did you sense that the owners of this home cared more about it than, say, the owners in the above paragraph? Did you make sure that you, too, stayed on the path of the brown paper, not straying because you did not want to mess up the rest of the home?

Do you believe that someone who takes the time to protect the floors in this manner would take much pride in the building? Do you think that owners who are this meticulous would take equal care regarding the myriad details required to keep a building in top condition? Are you more impressed by a home with brown paper than one without?

The apartment manager applies this paper to every vacant unit being shown. The manager swears by it. The manager procures three-foot wide rolls at carpet or art supply stores. After showing the units, they don't look like they have been visited by 5000 camels.

Because of these two tricks--magic scents & brown paper--people return to this complex and rent the units, keeping the vacancy level at one of the lowest in the area. The complex is located in a turbulent neighborhood between two major colleges. There is *always* high turnover in the area. The manager beats the competition, although the prices and amenities are not the most competitive. People rent because they perceive that the building is safer, cleaner, better managed and in better condition.

In reality, one could not ask for a worse building to manage. Something is always going wrong. It was not built well.

But perception is reality for many.

Every time it rains, the roof leaks. The upper floors get soaked. The light bulbs in the stairwells fill-up with water. The basement and parking garage flood.

The sewage lines are undersized. If people on the top floor flush their toilets at the same time as people on the bottom floor, then the bottom floor toilets overflow. The same thing happens with the garbage disposals and the sinks.

Doors are not squared. Windows do not close properly. Floors are not level. Marbles roll across floors by themselves...

For these reasons, is it any wonder why the manager has a higher turnover than normal?

Necessity is the mother of invention. Over six years of testing went into perfecting these methods. Units with paper were compared to units without. Units with scents were compared to units without. Units with both were compared...

You may try these tricks. But remember-- they're just tricks.

You might cause yourself a lot of future headaches...

HOW TO SAVE 1000 HOURS

This advice primarily applies to sellers who are selling on their own efforts. It can apply to anyone selling just about anything, but it is particularly helpful when one is selling a home. Once the technique is used several times, 1000 hours is not an exaggeration--it becomes a minimum over a few sales.

How many times have you placed an ad, only to have people call and ask the same questions over and over again? And how many times have you repeated the same answers? Isn't there a more effective means of communication?

Buyers do not like to play "tag." They are impatient. Money is in the hand to be spent, and time is precious. If the item is not available, they move on to the next one as quickly as possible.

When you run an ad for a house, much of your time and your buyer's time is wasted initially in attempts at learning the most vital points about the product.

This technique will not only save you time, but it automatically screens your potential buyers--bringing you the truly qualified, interested parties. You could place an ad in the paper with all of the information a buyer would need to decide whether he or she likes the home. You could mention the style, number of bedrooms, square footage, lot size, describe the floor plan, talk about the condition it is in, the flooring, the wallpaper, the location... But that would cost a small fortune! You'd have to sell the house to pay for the ads!

And most buyers would not read the ads anyway. They are impatient. When you are looking at a paper full of 100 ads, you don't want to waste five minutes reading just one. The clock is ticking. You first want to select the ads that sound interesting and then follow-up. No one wants to read for a few precious minutes, and then learn in the final paragraph that the home is out of reach-- that the price is too high, that the home will not be available for six months, or that the home should have been placed in the "rental" and not the "for sale" section of the periodical.

And besides, too much print can form an unreal picture of your home in the reader's mind. It may make great ad copy. But when buyers arrive, they get turned-off because the home does not look as good as they imagined. Those "four expansive bedrooms" may feel like four breadboxes. This happens to sales agents who place their own ads quite frequently. "New and exciting" for the agent is "old and uninviting" for the buyer.

No two people have the same "mind's eye." The nerve endings from the eye to the brain are much larger than from the ear to the brain. We remember pictures. We forget what people say. Perhaps you can't recall what many instructors discussed verbatim, but you can probably remember what they looked like.

"A picture is worth a thousand words."

But who wants to read a thousand words about your house? Time is money! And you just want to get the largest number of buyers interested in the property, see it, and go from there. You don't want to waste time answering the same questions about your home!

A photo ad will not answer the questions for you. It doesn't give enough information. And photo-copy consumes more space than print-copy. Consequently, it is more expensive. For the money, it is better to go with several small print ads that generate interest and phone calls rather than with exotic, expensive one-time ads.   Use ads such as:

> Stunning Modern. 3 + 3 + maids, 10% under market, xlnt area, high assumable. (xxx) yyy-zzzz.

That's all you need in an ad. Just enough to create interest and generate calls. Truthful. Realistic.

Now for the technique. When the calls come in, your answering machine gives them a professional sales pitch. It's automated. Timesaving. Paints an image but not a detailed picture. Doesn't get boring. Easier to absorb than print. Relieves headaches. Screens the cranks. Brings you qualified buyers. How?

Here's a sample of the response. Suppose you just called regarding the "Stunning Modern" home, above. Imagine that you are listening to the following message. If you don't believe the technique works, have someone read it to you and observe your impression......

A voice comes on the line, speaking in a friendly but professional manner...

"Hello. You've reached the office of _____. I'm unavailable to come to the phone right now, but if you leave your name and number, I'll call you as soon as I can... If you are calling about the house..."

--Here, if you have a multiple answering device, simply ask them to key in the number for the house that you are selling. Or, they simply stay on the line for the following message:

"The modern home was designed and built in 1990 by renowned architect Francois Dubois. The home is set in the serene, woodsy Maple Canyon environment of Brentwood. The lot size is 12,000, and there is a quiet stream in back of the house from which deer often drink.

"The home is multi-level, containing three stories. The garages, maid's room with bath, gymnasium and laundry facilities are located on the first level. The second level contains a formal entry, living room, family room, updated kitchen, breakfast nook, half-bath and terraces. The third floor contains the three bedrooms and two more bathrooms. There is also a rooftop garden. There are fireplaces in the living room, family room and mastersuite. Total square footage is 4475.

"The loan amount is $zzz. It is assumable at 1%. The monthly payment is $www. The price of the home is $yyy.

"If you are interested, please drive by 1414 Maple Canyon Road. Or if you'd like to see the home, please leave a message requesting an appointment to see it. Again, that's 1414 Maple Canyon road, just off Sunset between Bouregard and Bourbon Lanes.

"Thank you for calling."

How much fluff is in this ad? It's straightforward. Strictly business. You can write your ad the same way. And it will sound professional.

If you feel uncomfortable about giving out the address, then leave it out. Including it usually saves additional time. People who call again after driving by are often fine, seriously-interested people.

How would you like to read the above house description to every prospective caller who answers your ad? No thanks?

That is what you usually do unless you use this technique. You spend a minimum of five-minutes chasing every call. After a few newspaper ads, that adds up to a lot of hours. Be creative. Apply this knowledge the next time you try to sell something.

THE "THREE BLINDS"

What three factors contribute very little toward selling a home?

What three factors do sellers believe are the most critical to enable a home to sell?

Are the items the same?

Yes--indeed they are.

For this reason, the items are occasionally referred to as the "three blinds of sellers"--because sellers only see these three things.

The three factors are:

1. Signs
2. Open houses
3. Advertising

A seller sees a sign in the front yard of the home. Now everyone who drives by will know the home is for sale.

The open houses attract the public. A buyer will enter the house, or perhaps the home will become a "hot item" through comments of people who visit. Tell a friend...

And with ads in the local papers, all a seller has to do is to sit back and wait for every buyer in town to stampede across the lawn and charge through the front door.

Whoa! Don't believe what you see. According to national studies, these factors contribute to the sale of a home as follows:

	Study 1	Study 2
Signs	15%	17%
Open houses	3%	-
Ads	7%	15%
Total	25%	32%

And if there is a glut of similar homes in your area, then these figures drop substantially.

If it is a "seller's market," then all you have to do is to place a sign in the front yard, run a few ads in the local papers, and conduct open houses regularly, passing out as much information on the home as possible. Then, according to the above statistics, you have at least a one-in-four or one-in-three chance of selling the home. And count on doing this at minimum for the average number of days homes like yours are available for sale (i.e., "average days on market")...

If you don't like these odds, then you can see the necessity of finding an outstanding agent who knows significantly more about marketing your home.

For even if you use an agent, you can see that the above campaign does little to affect a sale.

Shouldn't you know in precise detail what else your agent is doing?

"MY CLIENTS WANT A HOUSE IN YOUR AREA"

The above line is a variation of the "I have a buyer" routine in the "Games" chapter on page 88. A derivative is "My client wants to buy a home in your neighborhood."

These are probably the safest all-time favorite lines that agents use when they go door-knocking. The line gives the agent prominence because the agent has the ability to affect a sale <u>now</u>.

So if one wants to sell, one should list with the agent right now! And before those "clients" go somewhere else...

If a seller later learns that those "clients" didn't buy anything, how can one blame the agent? The agent tried! It's not the agent's fault that the "client's spouse died" at the last minute, taking "the buyers" out of the marketplace for a home...

Isn't this a lot safer than for the agent to go out on a limb, saying "I have a buyer for <u>this</u> house"?

Usually those "clients" are real people that the agent is working with, but who are in a different price range, and the "area" that they are looking at can be as large as Texas...

If an agent really had a hot buyer for the neighborhood, the agent would first line up all the available homes, preview them, and then try to sell one.

PRICE RANGES

This discussion analyzes one of the most sensitive and critical issues in real estate: pricing a home. How do agent's shop for buyers who are in particular "price ranges"? And how can sellers price their homes to attract the greatest number of agents with these buyers?

Suppose, as a buyer, your income qualifies you for a $500,000 loan. You have a 20% or $100,000 down payment. Do you want to look at homes with a top price of $599,000? $575,000? $550,000? People don't get excited by buying less... So let's add information. Suppose the average price reduction on a $600,000 asking price is 10% or $60,000. If you pay full price on a $600,000 home, it may be *worth* only $540,000. Do you now want to look at homes with a top price of $625,000? $650,000? What if you could find a home overpriced at $700,000 worth $660,000 that you could buy for 595,000? Interested?

The point is that *agents* normally shop <u>above</u> a buyer's maximum purchase price for three reasons:

1) Houses rarely sell for their asking prices. When they do, usually the homes have been underpriced.

2) Real estate tends to appreciate. An agent who helps a buyer to purchase more today helps a buyer earn more tomorrow.

3) An agent who maximizes the purchase price also maximizes the commission.

Let's look at the other side of the coin.

Suppose as a seller you offer a home for $679,000. You are not getting a lot of activity. An agent recommends dropping the price to $669,000 in order to signal the market that you are a "flexible" seller. Why not drop the price to $659,000? Or better, lower it to $649,000? Referring to the above example, it might not seem like much of a difference.

Wrong. DEAD wrong. Here's the key. Agents are methodical. When they "pull" sets of homes for buyers, they use ranges of numbers in order to limit the scope of available homes. For example, if an agent has a buyer who can spend $600,000, the agent usually compiles a list of homes priced from $575,000 to $650,000 and then previews these homes to ascertain which ones fit the buyer's requirements. Please note the range in this example.

Why show a $675,000 home? If the house is overpriced, the seller probably has high expectations. If the agent presents an offer for $600,000, it will probably be rejected. To avoid this circumstance, agents stay within price ranges that have the highest probability of sale.

Let's ask another question. You are the seller. Your home is priced at $679,000. In what price "range" is the home for potential buyers? What criteria will agents use to select this home?

The vast majority of surveyed agents indicated that they like large, round, easy numbers. Below are examples of relevant ranges that agents use when they work with buyers ($ in thousands):

Maximum Purchase Price	Relevant Range	Maximum Purchase Price	Relevant Range
$ 100	75 - 125	$ 500	475 - 550
150	125 - 200	550	525 - 600
200	185 - 250	600	575 - 650
250	225 - 300	650	625 - 700
300	275 - 350	750	700 - 850
350	340 - 400	1,000	950 - 1250
400	375 - 450	1,500	1,400 - 1750
450	425 - 500	2,500	2,250 - 2750

When a seller's agent requests dropping a price from $679,000 to $669,000, the agent is doing nothing significant. As shown in the above table, the home is still in a relevant range for a buyer who can afford $650,000.

Seller beware! Is the agent promising, unrealistically, a selling price of $650,000? Has the agent overpriced the home from the beginning? Was it in the wrong price range? Is the agent afraid to admit a mistake? Did the agent "buy" the listing? Is the market changing? If so, why not move to the next significant pricing level, anticipating the market?...

"DROP THE PRICE BY $X AND REMAIN FIRM!"

When prices are dropping or a home has been on the market for a long time, an agent will often plead to drop the price for various "reasons" that sound quite logical:

> "It will send a message to other brokers that you're (the seller) flexible."

> "It will keep the home competitively priced."

> "It will make it the best deal in the neighborhood."

> "It will underprice the competition."

> "It will show that we have the most value for the money."

> "It will bring in offers--immediately!"

In all fairness, markets do change. If prices drop, one will probably need to lower the price.

In all fairness too, however, few people have ever seen or heard of an agent who said, "Prices are rising. Better raise the price by $X and remain firm." You'll probably never hear it, either.

Instead, here's what usually happens. Suppose a home was priced right three months ago at $499,000. Since then, the number of homes on the market has doubled, the number of people looking for homes has dropped by 50%, and now similar homes are coming on the market for $475,000. What should one do?

An agent says, "Drop the price by $24,000 and remain firm." Too bad the agent didn't anticipate this three months ago. Perhaps a seller was banking on that $25,000 for a trip to Tahiti. Now what? The seller drops the price to $475,000. Six weeks later an offer comes in at $450,000. How firm is "firm?" Two trips to Tahiti? Of course, the seller will probably counteroffer and settle somewhere in the middle.

The important point is this: any sales agent knows that "firm" is not forever...

HOW TO "JINX" A DEAL

"SOLD"

When an agent places this sign on a home before the deal closes escrow, a seller might start shopping for another agent--just in case. There is a higher probability than normal that the deal will not be consummated.

Agents love to place a "Sold" sign in front of a property once a house enters escrow. It broadcasts to all the neighbors a signal of success. It is proof that the agent has the savvy, talent and marketing skills to sell homes in the neighborhood. And if neighbors want to sell, they should list with the winner...

The broker feels the same way. It is a distinguishing mark for the company. Success breeds success. It is verifiable proof that the sellers have selected the right firm.

And the seller feels good, too. Every time a seller looks at the front yard, the "Sold" sign is proof positive that he or she made the right decision. Neighbors' homes may still be for sale, but these sellers are moving! In plus-or-minus 30 days! You can't tell these sellers that they did the wrong thing!

Unfortunately, however, that little sign triggers *buyer's remorse*. Suppose that a week after entering escrow, the buyers come strolling through during an inspection. How do they feel? Great entry! It should be--they're paying for it. Great kitchen! It should be--they're buying it. Great family room! It should be--they're paying for that, too. Large and comfortable bedrooms! They should be--they will be paying for them every month. Good sized yard and pool. Great--another monthly expense...

You get the picture. In the buyers' minds, the thrill of the chase is almost over. The hunt is no more. The home is not becoming an asset but a liability. The excitement of shopping has left. Do they really want to do this?

The responsibilities sink-in when they see that one word: "SOLD." Reality, like the sun, sets in the mind's eye. Darkness starts to come upon them. All because of that one sign...

So leave the sign off until the deal has closed escrow. Use a "Sale Pending" or an "In Escrow" sign to keep the buyers motivated. Neighbors can see that the house has been sold when the furniture is being loaded into the moving van.

FSBOS: HOW TO SPOT A BUYER FROM AN AGENT

Suppose that you are conducting a For Sale By Owner, selling your own home.

Here's another quiz. Spot the buyer from the agent in the responses below. Situation: you receive "The Phonecall." Someone wants to see your home! The doorbell rings. Greetings are exchanged. The other party takes a first step into the house, looks past you, and says:

     a)   Oh my! This is lovely!
     b)   Excuse me.
     c)   Wow! What a beautiful home!
     d)   Hello (second time).
     e)   Great curb!
     f)   Thank you (for opening the door).
     g)   Oh! And is that a fireplace I see?
     h)   Thanks (second time).
     i)   I love your decorations!
     j)   Nothing.

If you guessed a, c, e, g or i, then you spotted the agent. Congratulations! You should be in real estate!

Seriously... now that the agent has entered your home, you may as well ask for information. How is the home priced? How competitive is it? Does the salesperson have any real, living, qualified clients? If so, why not invite them over...?

It's always better to give a little away, pocketing 90+% of something than 100% of nothing.

PHANTOM SHOWINGS

Situation: your house is listed. Your agent requests that you prepare your house each time it is to be shown. The phone rings. Another agent wants to show the home to some clients in just two hours. Off to the races! You frantically:

a)   Do the dishes
b)   Pickup all dirty clothes
c)   Make the beds
d)   Change bathroom towels
e)   Clean all sinks
f)   Dust the furniture
g)   Vacuum
h)   Straighten knick-knacks
i)   Clean windows and mirrors
j)   Hose-down the garden
k)   Clean leaves, dead flowers, etc.
l)   And finally, turn on all the lights in your home

Then, with the other three minutes you have left, you shower and shave or put on your makeup, fix your hair and look stunning!

Whew! You made it! You notice that the agent and the clients are five minutes late. Where are they? You do some last-minute tidying-up. Suddenly ten minutes have passed. You watch through the front door. Twenty minutes. Thirty minutes. They'll be here. You try to do something else, awaiting strangers to pounce, invade your privacy and criticize your home. You're reading the paper, fidgeting. Forty-five minutes... Two-hours. You turn out the lights, cursing. You call your broker: "Leave a message, please." You call the clown who didn't show up: "Leave a message, please." And you do!

What happened? Where are they? How could they do such a thing--make an appointment and then not show up? Don't people respect your time?

After you hang up, you feel alone, frustrated. It happens all the time in the business... Three hours after you called the agent who made the appointment, the agent returns the call, explaining that:

1)   The client became ill
2)   The client was running late
3)   The car broke down, etc., etc...

So?

The agent feels that there is a legitimate reason, "apologizes" (i.e. explains), and hangs up.

But it's the third time this week! Different agents, same problem. Same lame excuses. How about something new, something truthful?

What can you do?

Wouldn't it be nice if, just once, an agent who is more than fifteen minutes late would call and tell you?

If one ever does, you might consider changing your agent for this one. Such courtesy typifies a *Rainmaker*, and is a hallmark of one's professionalism. It exemplifies glowing treatment that endears one to clients and to fellow agents, building cooperation which helps get your home sold.

Your best course of action, however, after being "had" this way, is to do the following:

a) When agents call to schedule appointments, inform them that you are a punctual person, reminding them to call if they are going to be more than 15 minutes late. And if you like, casually mention that if they will be late, they will not be allowed into the house because you will be "holding your monthly meeting for the Elephant Tribes of India Club and there won't be enough room to move..."

b) Take the agent's name, company and phone number. Keep a log of showing appointments. If the "no-show" stunt is pulled and the agent calls again--bingo!--you're ready! Let the agent have it!

GREAT EXPECTATIONS AND BROKER'S OPEN HOUSES

"I'll have 250 brokers at the open house!"

Yes--including Santa Claus and the Tooth Fairy? Don't confuse the Smoke of Sales from the facts: a good open house for brokers *might* attract 50-75 sales agents for a normal home that is new on the market--on a <u>spectacular</u> day. And unless the home is priced ridiculously low, few of these agents will have The Buyer, or any buyers, for the home.

If a sales agent boasts that he or she can attract 250 brokers or agents--or even any absurd number upward of 100--then either:

a)   the home is priced too low, or

b)   the agent is using gimmicks to attract other agents which will not result in a sale (see "Super-Commissions" on page 137 as an example).

Case example 221: an agent promised the magic number of 250 agents for a broker's open on a $3 million dollar home. She ordered caterers, champagne and violins. She sent personal invitations. She held the home open extra-long hours--from 10 a.m. to 4 p.m.--giving agents plenty of time to arrive.

Unfortunately, when only 52 agents arrived throughout the day, she had "caviar on her face." You see, this event occurred during a flat market when even seasoned, high-ticket agents were hustling to find buyers in the $100,000 - $200,000 price range. Not many agents had buyers in this higher-priced category.

It wouldn't have been so bad if some of these agents had buyers for this particular home. She would have "saved face" if this dismal turnout had resulted in a few showings to potential buyers. However, the seller found out that most of the support at the open house came from the agent's friends. Friends are wonderful for socializing, but they can't help much if they don't have buyers. The seller was a businessman. He fired her immediately.

Why? He said that he figured that if the lady was going to play "great expectations" with him from the start--resulting in nothing--then he could expect the same later on. Personally, he seemed a bit ruthless. But he wanted and knew how to get results. He also knew that if the agent was playing "great expectations" with him--that she was playing the same game with other agents, giving the home a bad reputation. Beware!

LOWBALL OFFERS - FOR SELLERS

In the following situation, the numbers may change but the situation occurs frequently. Let's assume that it just happened to you. What should you do?

You're angry. You're frustrated. Some dumb agent has just presented an offer for $600,000 for your home. You're home is priced right at $995,000, which also makes it the best million-dollar deal on the market. How should you react?

Relax. If you feel insulted, it's nothing personal. It's just a game and is no reflection on you, your home or the marketplace. It's the "lowball game." If you don't want to counter-offer and "dump" the property for around $800,000-- which is probably what the buyer wants--then simply, graciously say:

"I'm sorry, but it appears that your buyer cannot afford this house. Thank you for presenting the offer. Good-bye."

Enough said. With no counteroffer, you will make these charlatans appear like idiots, and they will know that they have wasted their time. You will feel happy because you are in control of yourself and the situation.

A good agent will pre-qualify a buyer. If the buyer can only afford $600,000, the agent should not be showing the buyer homes for one-million dollars.

The agent is required to present an offer immediately--any offer regardless of price. The agent feels that he or she is simply doing a job. Unfortunately, the agent is not doing a very good one. A good agent will counsel a buyer to be realistic, putting in an initial offer that shows seriousness and credibility, that has at least an initial chance of being accepted with some room for negotiation. If not, a good agent will tell the client to find another agent.

But sometimes an agent does not mind looking like an idiot, and it depresses morale in the industry. If you do decide to counteroffer and this same game occurs--at any price--follow this advice when terminating the transaction.

You'll feel like a winner.

HOW LONG SHOULD A SELLER LIST A HOME?

One month? Six months? Three years? How long does it take to sell a house? Or does one simply want a "standard" contract--say for 90 or 180 days? This is one of the most precarious and important decisions a seller can make. Yet few sellers know of its pitfalls. Its ramifications can make or break the sale of a property.

Many agents are devious in their tactics, conning a seller into signing the longest listing agreement possible. How about one for three years?

Such an agent, whom we'll name Willard, is sitting back at the office, staring into his coffee cup...and when anyone comes within earshot, he looks up madly, stares at the photo of the home on his desk and gripes: "I ain't got no clients! I ain't got no clients! All I got is this one little three-year listing! I ain't got no clients!!!" His broker would probably love to fire him--but can't because Willard is his wife's brother-in-law...

There are thousands and thousands of clients in the marketplace at any given time. Potential buyers? People don't want houses--they want deals! There is always someone in the agent's office who will buy a home if it is at the right price! And potential sellers? Nearly everyone will sell a home and buy one across the street if it has twice the square footage for the same amount of money. Good deals? No clients?

Willard probably told some Sucker Seller that the market is slow--real slow--and that the average selling time would take three years. What is he going to do in the meantime? Just put the home in the multiple listing service and wait for the magic moment?

The same holds true for one-year, six-month or less listings: there is no magic number. Any good agent will know within one month if a home has a *chance* of selling, and the agent should tell the seller this. Not any chance. A *good* chance!

Of course, no one really knows for sure...

November is a traditionally slow month in the business. A home may be sitting all summer long. "All the buyers bought by September," an agent might say, "so the kids could start school." Then BOOM! TWO offers on the same day--one cold and rainy day...

That is the nature of the business.

Case example 175: one offer came in from a judge, the other from a gay couple--both on the same day in November after the home was listed for sale for <u>57</u> days--with no offers until then...

So what does one do?

Go with a guy like Willard, above, for three years? Or wait to sell after obtaining a real estate sales or a broker's license? Or call "information" in Las Vegas and ask them to send someone, thinking that this might be a better gamble?

Let's look at the situation from another perspective.

The 83-year-old gentleman who contributed the insight for this selection happens to be one of the oldest, practicing real estate agents in the country. After being in the business for over sixty years, he noted that there is a strategy that definitely optimizes the chances for a seller.

First, how do most *agents* look at a listing?

From an agent's point of view, who cares how long the listing is for--as long as the house sells within the given period? After all, an agent is investing much unreimbursed time, energy and money marketing the home. The sooner it sells, the better. But no sale--no payback.

Brokers, on the other hand, are a little wiser. Ordinarily they have been in the business longer. Plus they are usually "administrative types": they run a brokerage, an office, and do not frequently work on a transaction basis. That is why they employ gung-ho sales agents.

Brokers look at statistics such as "average selling time." If the average selling time is 120 days, they certainly would prefer to have a listing for 180 days. That way, the odds are stacked in their favor. The "house" (i.e, brokerage) can't lose!

But what about the agents?

Let's say a seller doesn't list with Willard. Instead, a seller follows the advice in this book and finds a *Rainmaker*.

Suppose this *Rainmaker* is a woman who is a sharp, intelligent business-person. All of the agents in her office respect and admire her. They love working with her on transactions. They know that she doesn't play games or waste people's time. She is responsive and does what she says she will do. A star agent.

But what about the Willards in her office? They love to pick up their coffee cups, hop into the company bus and be driven to see new homes. It's exciting. It's fun. It's new. It's different. It's not like work!

There are many Willards in the industry. And how long do they remember a home? Usually ten days--tops. Unless the home is a virtual amusement park.

For this reason, the seasoned veteran who contributed these observations recommends giving no more than a 90 day listing. Afterward, list the home with another agency.

Unless a seller is working with a "star" and is completely comfortable, then a seller should follow this advice.

New, fresh homes in an agency receive the most attention from the agents. And buyers like to pounce on the new deals before anyone else, to jump on the "office specials."

Otherwise, the home is simply an old, stale house in the eyes of the agents in one office.

Too often, once sellers rotate agencies they hear an agent come through the front door at a broker's open house, saying: "Oh! Did this house just come out? *I don't remember seeing it before.*"

This situation recently occurred in a house that was on the market for over *two years* with different agencies.

So consider the "ol' vet's" advice. It has been time-tested over a 65 year period.

DON'T BE PETTY

The concept of "self" takes precedence over all others for many people. Attempts to augment and increase one's possessions sometimes dominate one's entire behavior. People become consumed by selfishness. When extensions of the self-concept are threatened, skirmishes erupt, most frequently to protect what is considered one's property. Hostility is usually the outcome because one party is viewed as "greedy." But in the span of our lives, we simply control things for a short period. The older we become, the more we see that the things themselves are not as important as the people or feelings that are associated with them, or the good that they can do for others.

What good is an old baseball mitt lying idly in the garage to an elderly man too infirm to use it, when his grandson could be romping around a field, shagging flyballs with the glove? How much more pleasure would the object then give to the old man?

Oftentimes people lose sight of these things. For example, consider case number 1974:

The buyer and seller had reached agreement for an older, modest family home. The house was in escrow. The home inspection had been satisfactorily completed. The loan had been approved. Everything was ready to close. The buyer liked the only bathroom. It had much charm from a previous era. Big window. Lots of light. View of a private garden with Douglas fir trees in the distance. The bathroom, too, contained much wood, including a hand-oiled oak vanity with a porcelain sink and an oak toilet seat and oak toilet-paper holder. The buyer believed that he was getting all of these fixtures. No written agreement indicated otherwise.

The buyer took his final walk-through the day before escrow was scheduled to close. He noticed that the owner had changed the toilet seat and paper holder to some cheap white plastic items. When questioned, the seller declared "it's my property!" The buyer called the seller a "cheap S.O.B." What else was he taking? Faucets? Doorknobs? His pettiness created bad faith.

The agents spent $27.33 to replace the items, quelling the fury. For a long time, the new buyer said that he remembered this experience every time he used the bathroom.

Too bad the seller wasn't wise, like the grandfather with his baseball mitt...

PUTTING A HOME ON PAPER

Interested buyers who walk through a home want information sheets to take with them when they leave, something to reflect on when thinking about the home in private. In the business, these are called "setup sheets." Unfortunately nothing is standard within the industry. Most agents try to place one attractive photo on one page, with as much relevant data as possible, and then also include some emotional verbiage such as:

"Knockout Santa Fe! Updated! Tons of storage! Show and sell! Your buyers will love it!"

Agents with lower budgets simply place the data on old photocopied pages. Many leave out pertinent information, such as square footage, lot size, etc.

And still others go overboard, producing elaborate color brochures and spec sheets, usually for upper-end homes. It's often amusing to line up the brochures for multi-million dollar homes in a custom development area. The brochures usually boast the same fine oak cabinetry, sub-zero refrigerators, microwaves, "smart-home" features, fixture companies... One wonders how "custom" the homes really are... The homes become too similar, touting the same dull paragraphs with insipid information. As though someone would select a home over another because of the make of a chandelier?

Buyers do not like to get bogged down in superfluous details.

There is one sure-fire way to produce an effective brochure. It takes a lot of work, more than any of the examples given above. But buyers love it. Surveyed buyers indicated that if they are sitting at home looking at three setup sheets describing three similar houses, they prefer the home with the sheets that includes the following information:

1) <u>The normal setup sheet with photo(s)</u>. As described above, this sheet should have the most striking, dramatic photo of the home. It should also include pertinent information such as lot size, square footage, etc.

2) <u>The features sheet</u>. This sheet helps buyers to recall items they overlooked. Organize features by room. If a breakfast nook has a fireplace and built-in bookshelves, mention this. But don't go overboard. Don't give the bookshelf sizes... Too much information is as useless as too little. If you have something really special, include another photo.

3) <u>The floor plan</u>. People like to walk through a home in private. Not while you are away--but on paper. It doesn't matter whether the floorplan is quirky. They can add or knockout walls at will. They like to do this. They'll spend more time on your house trying to make it work than on some competitor's who only gave them one cheap spec sheet with no photo.

4) <u>The lot plan</u>. People love to walk inside and outside the house with their imaginations. If they want to knockout a wall and add a room, where will they do it? The floorplan does not completely answer the question. Can it be done? Is there a tree in the way? And where do they place the tennis court? Better to have them draw on your sheets than to continue shopping for another home.

5) <u>The comps sheet</u>. Buyers want to know how your home stacks up against the competition. So tell them! If it is a good buy, mention it! Don't just give comparable listings. Tell the buyer that yours is a good deal! Buyers love to hear this.

6) <u>The financing sheet</u>. Existing loan information. Monthly payments. Taxes. Utilities. Insurance. Special assessments. Loan assumption fees. Owner will carry? Put it all in. You won't have to waste time answering these questions later. Such questions always come up.

7) <u>The location sheet</u>. Highlight the home on a map or Thomas Guide page. Then buyers can find the home anytime their relatives want to see it. Or if they have an appointment for a second showing, you don't waste time giving directions, and they don't waste time getting lost, which also means that you don't sit around wondering what happened to them.

Let's put the shoe on the other foot.

Most people would think they were getting better service if handed the above packet with a smile rather than a cheap information sheet and a slap on the back from some sweaty palm.

Unfortunately, 90% of the agents give people the "backslap" treatment. Not that this is bad. Everyone works within a budget and with time constraints. The packets described here take a lot of work. Why waste time and money developing a dynamite brochure?

And this is one mistake most agents make.

Most agents think that when you have an open house for the public, that you are obligated to give an information sheet to everyone who comes through the front door.

Remember the excerpt "Myths of Open Houses" in the Myths chapter? Who comes through the front door? The general public. And that can get expensive! Why waste money needlessly? Give 'em the sweaty palm!

If someone is interested in the house, let them ask for the information. They certainly will! A wife out shopping for a home, finding one she likes, will always want something to take back to show her spouse or friend. Let her ask!

It's better to give comprehensive brochures to two qualified people than fifty flimsy spec sheets to the general public.

OWNER'S SYNDROME

"Owner's syndrome" is a malady that strikes most of the population. In fact, in infects 90% of the people at one time or another who are selling something. It even affects people who sell things for a living--usually when they are selling something that they personally own...

The "illness" is not really contagious. But it can be spread, occasionally to friends or relatives who usually catch it "after the fact." The "illness" has the peculiar effect of "turning off" prospective buyers and formerly neutral agents, rendering them antagonistic. In order to fight the "illness," their heads become very hot.

How can you spot this "sickness"? You will see buyers walking in the opposite direction, arms flailing in circles, muttering words like "unrealistic" and "crazy." They tend to be very excited. What are the symptoms? Excessive pride, vanity... an inflated sense of one's possessions... a belief that what one has is not only "good" or "good enough"--but good for all. It is also characterized by a tendency to hang on to the past, to see things through a very small keyhole...

In any real estate transaction, the buyer feels that the most neutral and objective parties are:

1)   The agents, salespeople, third-parties;
2)   An owner selling income property;
3)   An owner selling his or her own home.

Investors know that people in category #3 are usually very touchy and can be a pain in the a--. One wife's canary wallpaper installed twenty years ago, or one husband's self-installed, fifteen-year-old kitchen tile are rarely items of envy for a new buyer. But they may be a source of pride to the owners. And when the buyer verbally wishes to "remove the wallpaper and replace the kitchen counters...," then the sparks fly. Feelings get hurt needlessly. All because of "owner's syndrome."

There is only one way to avoid it. Recognize that when you put something up for sale, it will no longer be yours. You are letting the cup pass... If someone wants to pour out the water that was in the cup and fill it with vinegar, by all means let them. Who cares what they drink? As long as they pay for the privilege...

FALSE HOPES

The following passages are specifically designed for people doing FSBOs (For Sale By Owners). Even if you never attempt to sell a home on your own, you should be aware of the chicanery that permeates the real estate business.

Suppose you have placed some ads in the local paper and a few choice magazines. Good house. Good price. The phone rings. A sales agent calls you and asks whether you are cooperating with brokers. Translation: if I (the agent) bring a buyer to purchase your home, will you pay me a commission?

It would be very foolish not to cooperate with brokers. Unless you are in the last $100,000 home in a one-million dollar neighborhood, you should welcome all the help that you can get selling your home.

But this angle is the agent's hidden agenda every time one calls an FSBO.

There is nothing wrong with this agenda unless the means for getting you to cooperate are devious. Are they? The next step is to ask to see the house. Why? To get a listing. The next step is to show the house. Why? To get a listing. If there is a genuine buyer--which there rarely is (see the "I Have a Buyer Routine" in the Games chapter on page 88)--then the next step must be to get a listing. There is nothing wrong with this.

However, at each step you always get pitched about the virtues of the firm and of the agent. That's OK, too. That's why they called. If the agent really does have a buyer, you should give the agent a one-client listing agreement. If the house is sold to that one real client, the broker and the agent get paid. They are protected. If they do not sell it, you can continue to sell the home on your own. You are not tied up with a listing agreement.

But if that particular buyer does not buy, what will the agent continue to do?

Right: "Pitch you for a listing."

And what happens when, after getting fed up trying to sell the house on your own, you decide to list with someone else?

"The other agent stole my client!" one agent will often tell everyone who listens...

"A clear-cut case of prestidigitation!"

Not too professional. But this "sour-grapes" routine happens. You get bad-mouthed by some disgruntled agent.

What you need to know is this: the above sequence of events happens every time and every other week when you are trying to sell your home by yourself.

Unless you are the only million-dollar home in a $100,000 neighborhood, all of the agents will call you...

Fine. There is nothing wrong with this.

But remember: it usually leads to false hope, high expectations, and no sale.

Or maybe--maybe--a listing...

WHAT TO DO WHEN YOUR HOME
IS OVERPRICED OR UNDERPRICED

Lower the price? Raise the price?

No, no, no, no, no... Those answers are too obvious. You know that you will be required to do this eventually. Let's discuss a greater concern.

How did the home come to be overpriced or underpriced? If it was through the error of an agent, then you have a big problem.

Let's look at a few case examples and their ramifications.

No. 82: Nina P. placed her home on the market for six months. She started at $695,000 in the summertime. As the market declined, she lowered the price. At the expiration of the listing agreement in November, the final price was $649,000. Agents called Nina immediately upon learning that the listing had expired. They naturally asked Nina for a listing. The new suggested prices were $600,000 and above. All of them fell below the last listing price. Agents don't like to take listings at the last asking price. It's "bad luck." If the last agent couldn't sell it at that price, how can they?

Enter Agent A. The agent was extremely well-known and respected in the area. Agent A and her partner saw nothing wrong with the way the home had been previously priced. For what the home had to offer compared to the other listings these agents had in their portfolio, the price seemed fair and reasonable. They recommended to Nina that she keep the price at the same level: $649,000.

Nina listed the home with Agent A in December. The agent had told Nina what she wanted to hear.

The holidays were slow, as usual. Few people like to move at Christmas.

In early January, Nina received a phone call from Agent A, who stated that several of the other agents in her office had seen the property. The other agents felt that the home was overpriced and would not sell. Agent A apologized, recommended a price reduction to $599,000, and left the decision in the hands of Nina. Agent A was sure that the home would sell quickly if this suggestion were followed. Either way, Agent A supported Nina with any decision that she made.

So, Nina dropped the price to $599,000. She felt bitter. Understandably.

Four months later when the listing expired, the home still had not sold. Toward the end of the listing period, Agent A again apologized, noting that the market had slowed after Christmas. Agent A felt that if the home had been priced originally at $599,000 it would have sold before the new year.

What should Nina do now? What about lowering the price a bit? It's Nina's decision, Agent A told her. Lower the price and leave it on the market for a while longer. It will sell. Either way, it's Nina's decision. The agent will do whatever Nina wants...

And what about the story of Mrs. S? Case example 38: seventy-eight-years old, living in the same home for forty-two years, right on the corner in an area zoned for apartment buildings.

Her broker showed her his personal market analysis and signed her for a 90 day listing, saying that it would be priced right at $250,000. The agent's partner then made an offer and purchased the property.

Almost before Mrs. S had packed and moved her things onto the street, the broker and his partner had obtained city-approved plans for a four-story condominium project. The lot should have sold for no less than $*400,000*.

In both cases above, the sellers protested to the local realty boards. What can the boards do? They could revoke licenses. But why? Mistakes do happen, markets do change, and the sellers did approve prices and price changes. Take the issues to court? Very costly.

Whenever you talk to a lawyer about real estate, the lawyer will normally say one thing: "It looks like we have a good case here!"

And you can hear the cash register jingling. Not for the money that *you* will collect, but for the lawyer's fees...

These sellers made the mistake of not relying on the weight of collective opinion.

No squirrel gathers its nuts from only one tree: the squirrel would not live very long. Seek out the *unbiased* numbers of *several* agents, throw out the highest and lowest numbers, and select a conservative one.

For added good measure, look at the selections in this book titled "Price Ranges" and "Case Example 217: How to Sell a Home in Any Market." You want to develop a cohesive *pricing strategy*, not just a number.

When the home is overpriced or underpriced for no rhyme or reason, as in the above examples, a seller should do one of three things:

      1)   Fire the agent!

      2)   Fire the agent!

      3)   Fire the agent!

A seller may also register a complaint with the local realty board.

It might help the next victim.

Do these things immediately. Protect yourself!

Why should the agent be fired immediately, besides avoiding such aforementioned outcomes?

Think about what a gross error in judgment means on one of the most important transactions in a person's life, and on the most important part of the transaction. Either your agent is trying to bamboozle you, or your agent is simply an ignoramus.

Either way, you get hurt! Seller beware!

CLIENT OR COMMISSION?

When the going gets tough, how much support can one expect from an agent? The "acid test" always involves money. Here is a quiz drawn from a recent event that happened to a seller, case example 3977:

A seller listed his property with a broker. The seller's agent continuously re-iterated that she wanted what is best for the seller. The seller has three options regarding the property--and can't make a decision. Please select what you believe to be the best choice for the seller:

1) Exchange the home for one that is lower-priced, incurring a tremen-dous tax liability because of the capital gain. The agent would net a double commission--one for the sale of the home, one for the effective purchase of another.

2) Cancel the listing. The seller was working on a deal with someone he knew before the listing began. The seller can exchange the home with this person for a higher-priced but inferior-quality home that has rental income. No commissions would be paid in this transaction.

3) Cancel the listing. Keep the current home, slowly going broke. The seller is over-leveraged and has cash flow problems.

4) Continue listing the home with the present agent, hoping that a buyer will soon appear.

5) Change agents.

Tough choices? What choice?

What does the agent want?

    a)   Whatever is best for the seller;
    b)   A commission.

When the seller felt pressure from the agent to make choice #1, the seller did the right thing: he made choice #5, changing agents, continuing to list his home, praying for the right opportunity before the bank foreclosed, leaving open option #2 to trade-down to a lower-quality home with rental income.

Seller beware!

OPTIONS TO BUY

This selection addresses one of the most damaging practices in the industry.

Suppose you contact me to appraise a 10-carat diamond ring, telling me that you intend to sell it. I know that the ring is worth a fortune, but I err on the conservative side. I appraise it low. Very low. Very, very low. Then, knowing that you are selling the ring, I ask for an option to buy it--at this low, low price. I even ask you to sign a piece of paper authorizing the fact that I am being granted the right to buy the ring, acknowledging that I could make a profit on the deal.

What do you think I'll do next? I'll run, or better, *fly* to every "investor" I know, trying to sell it. Or--I'll buy it myself.

Agents are allowed to do this all the time. They perform a market analysis on a home, and then make pricing recommendations.

Supposedly, agents can lose their licenses for pricing a home too low or too high.

But "too low" and "too high" are vague definitions, especially when numbers can lie because assigning values to comparable homes is a *very* subjective process.

There's only one thing better in real estate than a commission for an agent-- and that's profit. Plus, when an agent buys and sells, the agent doubles commissions. This practice is completely legal. Does an agent have incentive to undervalue a home?

There is only one way to protect a seller: obtain comparable values from different agents and go inspect the "comparable" homes.

And beware the "option to buy" game from your own representative...

STALE HOUSE SYNDROME

When is a house stale? It's not just when the windows haven't been open for three days...

Case example 1809: Sandra D. listed the home, which she co-owned with her mother, for sale with an agent for <u>six months</u>.

The first few weeks were exciting--open houses for brokers, open houses for the public, feedback, readjustments in the marketing plan... Everything was new...

Three months passed. A low offer was rejected. Another month passed.

By then, nearly everyone was familiar with the house. The other agents had seen it, or at least those who had had buyers for this particular neighborhood and price range. The agent certainly knew the house. Hundreds of hours had been poured into the sales campaign, as well as substantial sums for advertising, luncheons, returned inquiries...

Sandra sensed that things had quieted down, and she wanted to see some more activity on the home--more showings, more ads in newspapers, more flyers... She asked her agent to get busy.

Have you ever given two-weeks notice on a job? If so, how long did those two weeks seem? Eternity and back? How hard did you work during this period? If you are like most people, probably not much.

The same motivation occurs when a house becomes stale for an agent. It usually begins after the half-way period in a listing. For example, if a house was on the market with another company and the new agent has signed a three-month listing agreement, the house will feel stale to the agent within six to eight weeks. The odds appear to be against consummating a sale.

What are the games? Sandra approached her agent three different times in the fourth month with requests. Here are the responses:

> "Well, Sandra, I don't think we need to spend any more money on advertising. After all... all of the brokers in town know that your house is for sale..."

"Sandra, I'll hold another open house for the brokers if you want me to. We have a new agent in the office, and I can probably get him to sit the open house."

"I'll reissue the listing again if you want me to, Sandra. I don't think we need to send out flyers, though. They didn't draw much of a response the last time."

Only one type of advertising is effective: repeat advertising. Why discontinue the efforts?

The three answers from the same agent reveal how the agent feels about marketing the property.

In order to protect one's self from stale house syndrome, one must recognize the staleness as it is developing.

Sandra eventually fired the agent and found another, believing that the first agent could not overcome the attitude of overwhelming malaise and indifference.

After a short period, activity with the second agent also slowed. Sandra felt that the problem to be addressed was that the house seemed to be getting stale in the marketplace, rather than that the agent might be losing motivation. She approached the second agent.

Unlike the first agent, the second accepted Sandra's observations openly and calmly. And like Sandra, the agent also felt frustrated, and was relieved in discussing the problem with her. They sat down and brainstormed. What new marketing strategies could be applied? How could interest in the home be regenerated? Was there an untapped pool of agents or buyers who had not been solicited?

The combination of good communication, shared goals and creativity caused a lot of energy to be focused toward an unexplored marketing channel.

The house sold three weeks later...

RELISTING: THE "THEY SHOULDA" ROUTINE

Situation: a home was on the market. The listing expired. All the agents in town are now calling the seller. The seller invites a few over for interviews.

What one thing always happens?

"You shoulda..."

It's so easy to find flaws. They're like mother-in-laws.

"You shoulda..."

Most agents rarely pass an opportunity to criticize a predecessor's work in front of a potential client.

This criticism presumably empowers the agent with superior marketing skills. The new agent tries to appear more knowledgeable and experienced, duping a seller into believing that faultfinding and successive corrections will get a home sold.

Should a seller give the agent the listing? Not necessarily.

A seller might interview a dozen agents and take notes on how each agent would market the home, comparing strategies and programs, synthesizing the ideas and devising a master plan.

But when the seller later ponders which agent came closest to having all the right recommendations, usually it won't be the same agent whom the seller would originally want to market the property, for whatever reasons...

In the process, a seller discovers that specific marketing programs are not as important as the time and energy that will be devoted to a house.

If you are in this predicament, you will learn in the following chapter "Attributes of *Rainmakers*" how to select a good agent.

For now, remember that unprofessional agents take cheap shots.

IF YOU HEAR NEGATIVE COMMENTS...

A good agent rarely criticizes a home. Why?

> 1) It reflects a negative mental attitude;
>
> 2) It reflects badly on the agent's company.

Suppose your home is being shown by an agent and you overhear the agent make a few slighting comments.

Wallpaper is outdated. Floorplan is quirky. House needs more light.

Wait a minute! Who is this all-star? What's the agent doing showing the house if he or she doesn't like it?

Good question. Answer: either the agent is

> a) Selling another home, or
>
> b) A moron.

Why? The agent is giving clients excuses not to buy the home, which equates to reasons to buy another one that supposedly requires less repair.

Perhaps the clients liked your house and wanted to see it again. Perhaps the clients wanted to see similar homes in the neighborhood.

What to do?

Show all of them the door and call the agent's broker to register a complaint. Agents like this lower the morale of the industry and give it a bad name.

Don't take it personally. Both a & b, above, are the correct choices...

THE BITTERSWEET KISS

There are four basic stages of the seller-agent relationship. Think of the relationship as a marriage.

1) The courtship... There is nothing wrong with a home when an agent wants a listing: "It's <u>beautiful</u>. It could use a few changes... but what home couldn't? Have you ever seen a perfect home? It has charm, character, a warmth all its own..."

If a home was built by a known builder, or has much light or a tranquil setting--it will be mentioned by the silver-tongued agent as a "unique feature" that will be appreciated by buyers.

Even if the home is a dump with a rotten roof, termites, and is half-off its foundation--then it could be the opportunity of a lifetime for someone with a little talent, a little time, and a bit of elbow grease and weekend handyman skills to come in and turn it into a sparkling jewel. How many people wouldn't just love the chance to stumble across such a deal?

2) The honeymoon... Everything is new. The open houses, the advertising, even taking the measurements of various rooms. It's fresh and exciting. There is enthusiasm. You can feel the electricity in the air. Something's going to happen.

3) If the house is not sold right away, the newlyweds settle into marriage... Feet can smell... "Where are the results? Where is the rose-garden? Where are all the buyers? Where are the offers?"

4) On the way to separation... The intricate part develops when a bad offer comes in. Suddenly many agents say: "The home has a few rough edges. Those special qualities don't seem to be particularly important to the buyers... And many homes that came on the market since the listing began also seem to have similar features... It'll take more money than anticipated to put the home back on its foundation..."

There is only one lesson to be learned here from such sneaky, unprofessional agents:

First, they flatter you. Then, if they don't get what they want, they kick you in the tail. Beware!

FARMING

Let's look at "farming" from the standpoint of surveyed sales agents.

"Farming" is a term applied to a process for generating leads in real estate.

"Farming" involves making "cold calls," i.e., phoning or walking through neighborhoods, introducing one's self, soliciting potential buyers and sellers. Usually these neighborhoods are protected territories in an office. They are divvied between agents, enabling a firm to guarantee "coverage" for the area of town that the firm services. The area worked by an agent is known as one's *farm*.

Surveys reveal that in some cases an office will give exclusive rights to an agent within this farm. If Mary B. obtains a listing in John C.'s farm, the office will require that Mary turn over the listing to John. If this is not possible, perhaps due to the seller's protests, then the office will make sure that John receives a "referral fee" from Mary when the home is sold.

In other cases this custom is completely ignored. For example, it is not uncommon for several agents in a 100% commission office to solicit <u>one</u> high-priced home for a listing.

Surveys also indicate that the geographical size of the farm is insignificant. It could be as small as a few city blocks to as large as a given metropolitan area. Most agents like to handle between 500-1000 homes.

The process remains the same: cold calling. Hard solicitations.

One of the most common practices of farming comes when an agent acquires a new listing in a neighborhood. A card will be made saying something like "4444 Bloomer Lane! Another home listed with Gonzo Realty! Contact Jimmy D. for details!"

On one quiet Saturday morning, Jimmy D. will knock on doors, introducing himself, inviting people to an open house, attempting to acquire leads. The agent is getting "face time."

Surveys indicate that most agents do not like to farm in bad neighborhoods. Most agents hate to farm in hillside residential districts ("Oooh! My legs are killing me!"). And almost no one farms when it is raining.

Yet there are few experienced sales agents who do not take real delight in assigning a new agent the chore of farming in a hilly city like San Francisco on hot, blistering days... ("How'd it go today, kid?...)

How effective is farming? The consensus among surveyed veterans is that traditional door-knocking is no longer as effective as generating leads through bonafide contacts, such as business club membership, chamber of commerce meetings, personal interest clubs, church gatherings or direct mailings. Most agents feel safer with these other techniques, and say that they are more consistent referral methods.

Consequently, one rarely sees the "heavy hitters" of the industry walking through neighborhoods distributing flyers...

CHAPTER 9

ATTRIBUTES

OF

RAINMAKERS

By their fruits you will know them.

- New Testament, *Matthew, VII, 16*

In other sections of this book you have encountered the term *Rainmaker*, signifying an agent who demonstrates superior skills.

Many consistently successful agents have been studied over a ten-year period.

The traits and the habits which promote their success are shared in this chapter, as well as methods for separating the producers from the talkers...

RELATIONSHIP VS. TRANSACTION TREATMENT

The business of real estate is a personal affair. It is not like writing a check and having a nameless, faceless institution process the paper invisibly like billions of drafts each day.

The phrase "a person's home is one's castle" applies equally to rich and poor. From a king and queen looking for a new palace to a family looking for a starter home--most people exhibit zeal concerning their dwellings.

Successful agents indicate that real estate, like a legal or medical practice, is built on referrals and reputation. What is the best way to build the business? And what are the ultimate rewards?

One of the most satisfying experiences revealed by *Rainmakers* comes when, after several years of working with a client, the phone rings and an old, unfamiliar voice on the other end of line says: "Hello? Remember me? You sold us the home on..." After the voice expresses thanks and appreciation for the help and hard work, a request is made for the same personal attention in helping a friend or relative...

Case example 1701: a *Rainmaker* worked for a client <u>five</u> years earlier on <u>one</u> transaction, selling a home. The *Rainmaker* later changed agencies. The client phoned the original company and then the new one, tracking down the *Rainmaker* for another assignment. Was the *Rainmaker* pleased to receive the call?

Money alone does not buy the satisfaction of performing at one's best. To do a job well, to elicit this kind of response, people must be considered as *clients* and not simply as customers. Customers walk into grocery stores, usually meeting someone only when they are ready to exit in a nearly mechanical exchange. Clients are handled with kid gloves. The client who sought the *Rainmaker* after five years did so for one reason: "She treated me better than any agent I've ever had. She was courteous, polite, always returned my phone calls promptly, and even did things such as send me *Thank You* notes for minor reasons. She followed-up and followed-through."

Rainmakers conduct business with a long-run strategy. The "business" is viewed as working on a <u>relationship</u> rather than on a <u>transaction</u> basis. Many *Rainmakers* express that whenever they meet a client, they automatically assume that they will know the person five or ten years down the road...

FOCUSED

Rainmakers tend to be successful because they are *extremely* focused. Those who are not focused flounder, their business suffers, and customers loudly complain, expressing dissatisfaction due to a lack of results.

Being focused in real estate hinges on two key variables:

1. Knowing what one wants, i.e., a specified goal and a deadline for its achievement;

2. Allotting the necessary resources to accomplish this goal within the required time.

These factors, moving hand-in-hand, seem quite general and easy to apply. While most agents will say that they are focused, they do not understand how these two factors complement each other in the real estate business.

Let's look at some everyday examples.

Joe S. wants to list a home. Joe wants a 180 day listing. During an interview with Joe, the seller asks Joe how focused he would be if he were selling the home. Joe replies,

"Oh, *very* focused. After all, my listing agreement gives a set price for selling the home within 180 days. If I don't sell it, I lose a lot of money. How can I <u>not</u> be focused?"

Joe is half-correct.

Now suppose that a buyer is looking for a house with an agent named Bobby. Bobby doesn't know exactly what the buyer wants or precisely how much the buyer can afford, but has pledged to find the right home. Perhaps the buyer has seen a half-dozen homes with Bobby, and Bobby has a "ballpark range" of what is affordable based on rudimentary comments. When asked how focused one is, Bobby would probably respond:

"Very focused. I'm finding a house. I have a good idea of what my buyer wants and how much the buyer can afford."

Like Joe, this agent is also half-correct.

Let's introduce some real-world complexities into these examples.

Suppose Joe lists a home for sale and simultaneously has ten other listings. He has no assistant. Surveys indicate that *Rainmakers* with the happiest clients start to feel quite stressed when they approach a workload of ten listings. They feel that there just isn't enough time to service sellers adequately and to develop new business. How focused can Joe be under these circumstances?

For the first one or two weeks, Joe will probably seem very focused with respect to a property. Rooms will be measured, signs will be installed on the front lawn, ads will be written, spec sheets describing the home will be filled out, the home will be placed in the multiple listing service, a broker's open will be held, and perhaps the home will be open for the public and for the benefit of neighbors. Standard, initial marketing procedures.

Now what? How about the rest of the business and the complaining sellers who were ignored while Joe was busy toying with one home?

Let's look at this situation from another perspective. The listing period is for 180 days. Now that the listing is on "auto-pilot," how concerned will Joe be with the home in 120 days? As you learned in previous chapters, an agent tends to become less enthusiastic the longer a home is in the marketplace.

Only one type of marketing--like one type of advertising campaign--is effective. Repeat marketing. Repeat advertising. Continuous efforts. Continuous exposure. Joe should "get off the dime" and keep working.

Does Joe seem *extremely* focused on selling the home?

And from the perspective of Bobby who is working with a prospective buyer--could the agent be more focused if the agent knew *exactly* how much the buyer could afford and what the buyer wanted in a home?

How focused should an agent be? Let's look at the extreme cases.

Suppose Sally obtains a 90-day listing on a home. Sally works full-time in the business. She currently has two other listings: both are in escrow. In 21 days she will have no other listings. She really wants the business. She really needs to sell this next listing to stay out of debt. If she doesn't sell it, her family won't eat. How focused is Sally?

Suppose Sally hits the home run and places the home in escrow in 30 days. Suppose the sellers now need to move within four weeks. They are Sally's only clients. Sally knows their financial details. Sally also has a very, very good idea of what they want in a home because she has spent a lot of time in the present house, discussing likes and dislikes. How focused is Sally?

In both cases, Sally will allocate all necessary resources to get the job done. Results are what count for Sally. She has the knowledge and the motivation to succeed.

Somewhere between these extremes and the initial examples are all of the agents in real estate. As you can see, it is critical to understand how focused an agent will be in meeting a client's needs--and to determine what resources will be allocated to the client and *only* the client.

Some agents will say they are extremely focused because all they do is work in real estate: they have no other life.

But as you see, that may not meet a client's needs.

Specific goals, deadlines for their accomplishment, and the resources allocated to ensure the results...

A sales agent only feels as successful as the last transaction. Being focused enhances the probability of success.

The big goals--buying or selling--are comprised of many small steps. Most successful agents develop a set of realistic minor goals along with a timetable for their achievement. Then, they allocate resources and mark their progress. In this way, successful agents control *the process* that contributes to becoming and staying successful.

And the agents also gladly explain to a client the resources that will be dedicated to meeting the client's needs...

PRODUCTIVITY ANALYSIS

An agent's true capabilities are not reflected in statistics such as total number of listings, total dollar value of homes listed or sold, total dollar sales...

Better measures are needed to reflect an agent's *effectiveness*.

Let's look at both sides of the business.

First, suppose you want an agent to sell your home. After interviewing ten agents, you narrow the selection down to the top four.

What criteria are you using? Biggest car? Best "chemistry," i.e., someone with whom you have the best communication?

Just because an agent sells *you*--doesn't mean that the agent can sell your home.

For example, this passage is being written in an elegant middle-class home during an open house. The home is priced right at $549,000. Two similar--but not as nice--homes one-half block away are priced at $759,000 and $699,000. Same neighborhood. Same street. Smaller homes with less-desirable floor plans.

Agents are *flocking* to the home that is priced correctly, commenting that they will bring buyers, casually mentioning that they have not and will not preview the other two homes. Why waste time? The homes are overpriced, they reason.

Who listed the other homes? Well-respected, tenured agents who are stable and conservative, who appear rock-solid, mature and credible. Just like their sellers.

But the agents have used very old, very stale comparables to obtain the listings. Probably two-year-old numbers prior to an economic downturn.

Such agents like to acquire additional listings in the early spring. Then, as buyers come looking for homes during the next few months, the agents have more listings than others. They drop prices with a few flexible sellers into the range of reality, hoping that the drastic price reduction will attract the attention of other agents who have buyers. And, if they sell one or two homes, then they earn easy money and a comfortable living.

Later, the next family sees "high" totals, e.g., number of listings, dollar value of sales, or maybe just the agent's familiar name with a "Sold" sign in the neighborhood--and the family believes that they have found a winner.

This scenario didn't happen on this street, however. Only one of the three homes sold. The two overpriced listings expired; the sellers then took their homes off the market, frustrated by "deflationary shock."

Here's the best way to analyze an agent's effectiveness. Ask an agent to give you a breakdown like the chart below:

A	*B*	*C*	*D*	*E*
Listing	Original Asking Price	Selling Price	Ratio of Selling/ Asking	# Days On Market
49 Wagon Rd.	999,000	950,000	95%	61
15 Mill St.	350,000	315,000	90%	28
11 Tull Ln.	750,000	-	-	-
29 10th Ave.	650,000	625,000	96%	47
71 Cutter Pl.	495,000	500,000	101%	6

F	*G*
Activity Period	Sales/listing Ratio
Last 120 days	80%

This table gives the most critical factors needed to determine an agent's effectiveness. Let's analyze the main points in order of importance:

Item G: Four out of five homes or 80% sold. Not bad! That means that you have an 80% probability of selling your home with this agent, which is quite a high success rate. How does this compare to other agents being interviewed?

Item D: The high selling price/original asking price ratio shows that the agent valued the homes well, garnering very close to the asking price. It is better to believe this agent's suggested asking amount than someone who tries to talk you into an exorbitant figure that the market may not bear, later having to drop the price drastically in order to obtain a sale.

Item F: The activity period for this information should be recent--close to when you plan to use the agent. All listings should be included.

Item E: The number of days a home is on the market varies according to prevalent economic conditions. Compare this range with other agents. Which agent's homes are selling faster--or slower--than others? Why? Are the homes over- or underpriced? You don't want your home to be the "three-hour wonder" that sells the very first day because it is underpriced, or to be the "three-year miracle" that requires three years to sell because it is overpriced.

Item B: How many homes are similar in price to yours? If an agent sells twenty $100,000 entry-level homes a month, the agent is definitely a superstar. But perhaps not good enough to sell a $1,000,000 mansion. Different marketing skills and sales techniques are required for each.

There you have it: a seller's guide to objectively and quantitatively selecting an agent to list your home.

But what if you are a buyer?

Let's look at the other side of the coin.

Buyers are a finicky bunch, and they test an agent's patience. Finding the best agent is often like the proverbial camel trying to pass through the eye of a needle.

But there is an easier way.

Rainmakers usually:

1) Qualify you. Find out how much house you can afford. Then they begin to arrange for excellent financing <u>in advance</u>. All purchase decisions begin with matters financial.

2) Ask you many, <u>many</u> questions about likes and dislikes of a home-- <u>before</u> you see anything. Square footage, floorplan, number of bedrooms and bathrooms, general location... Also, what you <u>don't</u> like, e.g., neighbors with barking dogs...

3) Have product knowledge. Has the agent ever built a home? Does the agent know the difference between "cosmetics" and a "major rehab"?

4) Show you homes that fit the first two criteria, above, on the <u>first</u> outing.

Of course, a buyer should know what one wants. If you do, and item #4, above, doesn't happen right away--then find someone else! You are wasting valuable time! Someone might purchase your home before you get the chance to see it!

"LISTING" AND "SELLING" BROKERS

The industry phrase "listing versus selling broker" describes two predominant methods of doing business. Each contains enormous implications for the type of service one can expect.

The phrase is actually a misnomer. In almost all transactions a client deals with a sales agent. The agent's broker does not normally adhere to one of these methods: the broker's business and reputation would suffer--because business and the needs of the community are one in the same.

Many sales agents subscribe to a different philosophy. If one of these methods works well for the agent, he or she may continue to exploit it. Who cares whether the method helps everyone? The agent can always change firms if too many people complain. Reputation or community standing are not paramount, as in the case of the broker.

The methods are simple. A "listing agent" focuses on obtaining listings. A "selling agent" focuses on selling properties. Sometimes these agents work in pairs, one concentrating on obtaining an inventory of homes while the other concentrates on selling them. This partnership rarely lasts because, as you will see, there is an immediate conflict of interest.

The listing agent tries to obtain as many listings as possible. Twenty. Thirty. Two-hundred. The more the merrier. Why? The agent is playing a numbers game. If Agent A has ten listings and 50% or five sell, then that agent will not earn as much as Agent B who has 50 listings when only 20% or ten sell. With this production rate, Agent B can afford to hire an assistant and focus on what he or she does best: look good, drive a flashy car, and talk people into listing their homes because of feeble reasons such as the virtues of "Company X."

You'll be impressed by Agent B. Perhaps you've seen the name plastered on signs around the neighborhood. Perhaps you've received mailers that boast of 10 homes sold last month by Agent B in your area. The mailers often cleverly omit the other 448 listings that haven't sold, or the army of staff who must help the agent.

Many of the listing agent's techniques and strategies were discussed previously in the Games chapter, such as inflating the comparables to get a listing, which is the most common and damaging disservice. The agent often reasons, "Why not start the listing at a high price? We can always drop it."

But pie-in-the-sky is not eaten by giraffes. Overpricing a home has definite drawbacks, as discussed in previous chapters.

The other major problem is personal attention. Any agent with more than 10 listings knows that there are not enough hours in the day to maintain adequate communication with all sellers. Any item which has the potential of generating quick cash takes precedence over all the others. Some sellers will just have to suffer. An agent with 20-30 listings will say that this does not matter. Good communication and hand-holding are not in the listing agreement. But sellers using such agents soon feel that they have taken a number and are waiting in a queue...

These are the major pitfalls for sellers who use listing agents.

What about the drawbacks for buyers? If the agent has time to show you a house, you will undoubtedly be shown Agent B's personal inventory of listings before all others. And many of the prices will not be the best deals in town. Guaranteed.

At the other end of the spectrum, the selling agent is usually a consummate master of the inventory of homes in an area, knowing all the best deals, rarely taking listings, preferring to work with buyers. If this agent takes a listing, it will usually be done at a low price in order to expedite a sale.

A seller usually does not obtain the maximum sales price when working with a selling agent. But a buyer may have the best opportunity for finding excellent deals.

What is the consummate selling agent? Most surveyed agents say they would bow to someone who consistently sells 20-30 starter homes a month. Of course, such an agent would probably use some high-pressure sales techniques to affect these transactions.

These are the major pros and cons of each agent. They have their strengths and weaknesses.

How do you tell which agent is which?

The listing agent is reasonably easy to spot: simply ask how many listings the agent has. Is it double the number of any other agent with whom you have spoken? If so, then also ask how many assistants are available to support the agent, learning whether you might obtain good service.

The selling agent will be more difficult to discern: ask whether the agent prefers to work with buyers, sellers or both. If the agent only works with buyers, then you will have your answer.

Also, ask how many listings the agent presently has and how many he or she likes to have at one time. An agent who prefers no more that 2-3 listings usually prefers to focus on sales, not listings. And ask about a recent sales record over the past three to six months. If the agent sells ten homes a month but only averages 2-3 listings, then you have a selling agent.

A *normal* agent will plod along averaging 6-10 listings at one time, very concerned that all of them are priced well to sell, very concerned that all of the sellers are happy in order to obtain repeat business and referrals, very concerned that knowledge of inventory is kept high for any potential buyers or for sellers when homes are sold and they are ready to relocate, very concerned that one is perceived well by one's fellow agents and by the community.

This is the attitude of a *Rainmaker*. It is very similar to that of a broker.

"Listing" and "selling" agents do not suffer the same pains of conscience.

PERSEVERANCE

Perseverance is like the engine of an airplane: no agent soars without it.

People in residential real estate are a special breed. After a few short and intense years, many of them beg to be committed to an institution because of the tremendously high level of frustration that comes with the business... Joking aside, one must continually pick one's self up from the emotional floor, the grief, the aggravation, the roller coaster of tension and stress from the ups and downs of the business...

Residential agents, as a rule, do not deal with companies. They deal with the least-sophisticated sector of the real estate industry. Most buyers do not even know the basics of finance and construction. And no seller, as much as he or she might believe it, has a perfect home. The setting is automatically rife with misunderstanding and an air of distrust. Through all of this, the agent must have the patience of Job and the communication skills of a diplomat.

Perseverance and hope are the ingredients that allow one to keep picking one's self up, to kick one's self high and often enough to climb the ladder of success.

How do you spot the trait of perseverance?

A *Rainmaker* will continually communicate with a client. The client's name will be placed on a "tickler file" for reference and action in the weeks and months ahead. Any commitment to action will be followed-through.

It is extremely important to spot the virtue of perseverance from the vice of being a nuisance.

For example, suppose a referral has been given to an agent through a mutual friend. The agent calls and attempts to develop a business relationship. The new prospect deals with the agent for a short period, discussing a few ideas, and then changes plans.

The agent keeps calling. Not wishing to be candid and forthright, the prospect tells the agent that he or she is not interested "at this time," hoping that the agent will go away. The agent keeps calling. Now the prospect resents the agent for not respecting one's privacy, and would like to tell the agent to crawl back under his or her rock. Instead, the prospect is polite, and continually invents excuses. The agent keeps calling.

In this scenario, which is presently happening to Mrs. Chandler during this writing, the agent is acting out of ignorance, not <u>hearing</u> the needs of the client.

Case example 4092: Mrs. Chandler listed a very expensive home with Agent P. After four weeks, the home was withdrawn from the marketplace. Agent P lost a lot of money incurring heavy upfront marketing costs. Mrs. Chandler now feels obligated to re-list the home with Agent P when selling conditions improve.

Enter Agent Y. Mrs. Chandler was referred by a mutual acquaintance. Agent Y phoned Mrs. Chandler, and Mrs. Chandler explained her situation, expressing that she feels obligated to relist with Agent P. Nevertheless, every 2-3 weeks Agent Y keeps calling Mrs. Chandler. Mrs. Chandler has never met Agent Y.

This behavior is not perseverance.

Case example 1314: Agent N began working for Mr. & Mrs. Lindblade at Christmas, trying to find them a home. Agent N looked high and low for her very finicky clients. Like many buyers, they wanted a castle for the price of a doghouse. But Agent N finally found the home: she earned her money.

That is perseverance.

Case example 326: Agent S listed the home of Mrs. Verst for sale. The home was a special-interest model that appeals to artistic people who like authentic homes in the Victorian era.

Agent S did not simply place a sign in the front lawn, put the home in the multiple listing service, and then pray that a buyer would magically appear. Instead, the agent drove weekly to all of the local real estate offices (including competitors), telling them about the home; advertised the home repeatedly in special-interest, artistic periodicals; passed-out flyers to a Victorian home society; and, pitched the home regularly at major realty meetings. The home finally sold to a special-interest buyer.

That is perseverance.

PROFESSIONALISM

An agent who does not conduct business professionally probably cannot conduct your business. The agent won't be perceived highly by colleagues, winning the utmost cooperation from other professional sales agents.

Expect low-key, high quality, understated elegance with attention to detail.

Rainmakers are reminiscent of the IBM sales force from the '60s--who wore blue suits, white shirts, shined shoes... Ready, willing and able to serve your needs.

Flashy cars are not too important.

Just a smile and substance.

INTEGRITY

Integrity means a lot in the real estate business because, unfortunately, it is seldom found.

Too many hungry agents stand in front of broken door knobs while showing a home. Even books by prominent real estate advisors with their own talk-show programs, for example, advise people with damaged hardwood floors to "try an old real estate trick: cover the damaged floor with a throw-rug."

Integrity means dealing with a company known for its honesty and reliability, for its staying-power in the community.

Integrity also relates to how other agents perceive an agent. Do they like to deal with that individual? Do they look forward to working with the agent on transactions?

If the agent works with a firm, then the office manager will gladly share information about the agent's reputation. Or, you can speak with the local escrow company with whom the agent normally does business. Or ask for names of recent clients...

ATTITUDE

Remember the goal of Benjamin Franklin? He sought to make his personality as "comfortable as an old shoe," eliminating all expression that causes discord.

The image goes a <u>long</u> way toward describing what a real estate agent needs to be successful...

LISTENING SKILLS

Some people are impressed by agents who seem to have all the pat answers, who "walk and talk like an encyclopedia."

Case example 17: Mrs. G interviewed an agent who had a doctorate. The agent spoke for half an hour. Non-stop! About "the market," the economy, the house, what the woman needed to do... He knew it all!

But something was missing: the personal touch.

Mrs. G was extremely impressed with the agent and his knowledge. At least until he returned with the listing agreement, which stipulated a six-month listing. Mrs. G wanted to go to Europe for three months, and then list the home for three months in the spring when she returned. She wanted no one to enter her home while she was away.

The agent may have <u>listened</u> to the client, but he failed to <u>hear</u> her needs. Instead, he interpreted his own needs--a six-month listing--and transferred those needs to the seller.

Too often agents make assumptions without taking the time to understand what is best for a client.

It is better to have an agent ask intelligent questions and take notes than to regurgitate a canned sales speech.

Isn't that what you would expect of a good employee?

DON'T UNDERESTIMATE THE UNDERDOG

Here's a story which illustrates the importance of not confusing style with substance. Case example 2149:

Agent J is well-known and respected in his community. He can usually be seen driving a new Porsche and sporting an attractive "assistant" on his arm. He operated his own firm for awhile, then sold it for a lucrative profit, choosing to work for a larger firm as an agent rather than dealing with administrative headaches as a broker.

Evidently, J knows the business. He promotes a wide-range of homes in a vast area and has many listings because of his name and "generalist" approach. He'll list any home.

J works using the "pyramid method." He overprices listings, promising to gain the most for his sellers, taking on as many listings as possible to garner market share, hoping that a few sell each month in order to maintain his image and lavish life-style.

One seller who used J became very disappointed when her home was reduced in price 15% over a six-month period and still did not sell, having become stale and overpriced in a crowded marketplace.

When the listing expired, she sought new blood and enthusiasm. She wanted an agent who would personally conduct open houses rather than J's hired "mannequins" who were paid by the hour to greet newcomers--but who had all the pizazz of a door mat.

So, she hired Dan. She liked Dan not because he was an ex-professional baseball player, but because he seemed to possess business acumen and marketing skills. He conducted himself as a professional. He only had three other listings at the time and no known name, but at least he worked for a reputable firm, she reasoned. She gave him a chance.

Instead of allowing the home to sit in the multiple listing service, Dan marketed the home like a tiger. He was hungry--very hungry. In two weeks the home was leased long-term for 20% more than comparable market rents. The seller was ecstatic, choosing to lease instead of selling in anticipation of a more favorable economic climate in one year's time.

Results are what count.

Surveys indicate that people want an agent who has business acumen, who communicates well and often, who keeps the client informed, who has time for the client and the client's needs, who has an understanding of what a client wants, and who looks out for the client's best interests.

What is more important? To walk into an agent's office knowing that your name is buried somewhere in the agent's files? Or to see your name and house pasted on the wall next to a hungry agent's desk and telephone?

Go with the tiger.

CONTINUING EDUCATION

Rainmakers know that success and knowledge go hand-in-hand in real estate. For this reason, they continually devote segments of time to bettering themselves, such as by attending courses designed to expand their horizons and to keep abreast of developments in the field. Many also consider their cars as "classrooms on wheels": spare moments are wisely utilized listening to motivational tapes or discussions from a recent seminar. Like the car, the education is viewed as a vehicle--but one which can be used in maintaining an edge over competitors--a means to provide better service.

CONTRARIAN VIEW

Seasoned agents like to analyze trends. They like to see where "the action" is headed so that they can get there first. Since business runs in cycles, a favorite forecasting device for a *Rainmaker* is other agents. Over the years *Rainmakers* have created the following saying to monitor their own behavior, comparing their present efforts to the trends of co-workers. In this way, *Rainmakers* determine their own direction and prepare for a change in the business cycle...

> When all the agents are accumulating listings,
> the wise agent accumulates buyers.
> When all the agents are accumulating buyers,
> the wise agent accumulates listings.
> How wise is your agent?

AREA SPECIALIST

There are many segments of the residential real estate business. Some people sell land, some sell loans, some specialize in certain types of homes...

The recommendation from a friend who "knows somebody in real estate" may be for a person not appropriate to serving a client's needs.

If your arm is broken, why visit an Ear-Nose-&-Throat doctor?

Surveys indicate that people selling homes want an agent who is a consummate master of their house, their block, the homes in the neighborhood, competitive houses for sale, why the home is better or worse than others, what schools are available, the reputation of the area... People reason than only an agent with this knowledge can counter any objections that arise:

"Yes, that third child's bedroom may be small, but it is larger than the home up the street priced $20,000 higher."

And the surveys indicate that people who are buying a home in a particular area desire the same mastery over details.

Some agents are good enough to meet a client's needs regardless of the assignment. The agents have the qualities described in this chapter. *Rainmakers* take time and effort to become fully steeped in the problem at hand, researching the answers of a specific concern from all angles.

Unfortunately, most agents are lazy. If a client wants to move to another area of town and the agent who sold the home volunteers to help, often the client's agent will simply call another agent in the new area and gather information. Then, when the client is ready to look, the primary agent takes the client down the path of least resistance, looking at homes which generally fit the client's needs and garner the highest commission. And usually the homes that are seen with such an agent--are seen for the first time together!

Very rarely will the agent pack-off and spend days or weeks in search of a solution to a client's problem, obtaining the best possible deal.

Make sure that the agent has mastery over the inventory of homes. And hopefully, the agent will be an "old grizzly" who knows the history and trends of the area...

PRODUCT KNOWLEDGE

Case example 501:

In one small corner of this world we observe Bill N., a.k.a. "Pops," practicing real estate, a consummate *Rainmaker*. Although he didn't obtain his real estate license until after he retired, Pops learned a lot about the business along the way.

Pops doesn't work with just anyone. But if you are fortunate enough to enlist his services, you feel like one of the blessed.

Pops had been a general contractor before he retired. He designed and built homes of many styles, ranging from traditional, California ranch, Cape Cod, Spanish, Georgian, and modern.

Pops obtained his college degree in engineering many, many years ago. He liked numbers.

Before entering the construction field, Pops worked as a branch manager for Bank of America. At the bank, Pops learned about loans, fiduciary law, customer service and marketing to small businesses and everyday consumers.

More important, after living on earth for many years and passing through many stages of different careers, Pops learned the value of helping people. He took great pride in helping find the right product--especially for first-time buyers.

If "markets" went up or down, it didn't affect Pops. If interest rates went up or down, it didn't affect Pops.

Through thick and thin Pops was there to do what is the core of the business: talk to people and help them solve their problems. Consequently, people were always calling with referrals or for advice. Clients that Pops had not seen in ten years still referred him business.

Pops had "product knowledge."

When you went out to look at a home, you didn't need to take a home inspector with you. Pops could tell you whether it was built well, and probably who built it and when. And because of his creativity, he could also "see through walls," i.e., understand precisely how walls could be moved and floorplans enhanced.

And Pops always knew approximately how much this work would cost.

Matters financial were no mystery to Pops, as they are to most real estate agents. He did not need to refer you to a third party in order to calculate how much money you could borrow. Simply give him your personal financial information and he could evaluate your credit standing by running the necessary reports.

After spending a few moments on his calculator with up-to-date information from a broad range of lenders, Pops knew almost to the penny how much your monthly payments would be.

When Pops told other agents that he had a good home that was a good deal, they <u>knew</u> it was a sound investment. Pops had credibility.

Pops also had integrity. If a house had been for sale for a year, he didn't tell people that it was only "on the market for three months"--which may have been correct--with the current agent! A home stood on its own merit or not at all.

Product knowledge: construction, law, finance and marketing.

Shouldn't an agent who tells you a home is a "good house" be qualified to render such a judgment?

NETWORKING

An agent who is selling a home relies at least 50-75% during all transactions on other agents to bring the buyer who will purchase the home.

Similarly, an agent working for a buyer tries to find "good deals" for the client before everyone else. And what is the best way? By "word of mouth."

Consequently, an agent's biggest asset is a broad network of top-quality co-workers. And there aren't too many ways to develop this. The best method is given below:

> - have many years in the business;
>
> - be considered a person of high integrity;
>
> - have a reputation of offering good value for the
>   money;
>
> - be cheerful and pleasant to work with;
>
> - do the little things that endear one to other people,
>   such as sending personalized *Thank You* notes
>   when another agent visits a listing;
>
> - conduct one's self in a professional manner, not
>   wasting productive time on such things as gossip.

These are some of the seeds an agent needs to sow in order to grow a business.

Let's look briefly at case example 1870: Alex L. was 30 years old, working as a waiter. The humble work taught Alex a valuable lesson: if you treat people well, they will tip you.

Alex sought an avenue for increasing his earnings. He read daily of growing real estate activity in his area. He changed vocations, hoping to succeed.

The first year was a struggle for Alex. He was relatively unknown, unskilled and unfamiliar with the inventory and the business. But Alex persevered.

And fortunately, Alex possessed a quality that endeared him to clients and to fellow agents. When people spoke with Alex, he gave them 100% of his attention. Clients and agents commented that they felt they were being treated as though they were Alex's best friend--regardless of how long they had known him.

In his third year, Alex leased a new Mercedes and a car phone, along with other emblems of success. He was earning in excess of $100,000 a year during a severe recession, an amount that was then quadruple the average American wage. He was considered a "heavy-hitter" in his firm and in the industry.

It didn't take long for Alex to succeed, to become a *Rainmaker*. He had acquired several of those characteristics described, helping him to establish a broad network of clients and fellow agents...

CHAPTER 10

TOWARD

CLEANING

THE

INDUSTRY

We demand that big business give people a square deal.

- Theodore Roosevelt, Letter

CHANGE THE LICENSING/EDUCATION REQUIREMENTS

The scene: a small auditorium. Approximately fifty people are seated listening to a keynote speaker.

"How many people..." begins the old white-haired gentleman. He has been asked to address this group because of his 35 years of industry experience, of which 25 have been spent on the Grievance Committee...

"How many people believe that there is a problem with this transaction... Suppose you, the woman on my left, have been showing properties to some buyers for about three months. You've shown the buyers at least two or three dozen homes. Finally, they find one they like, but they tell you that they are unsure. They want to think about it.

"So they go home and that weekend call up and have lunch with a good friend of theirs. Their friend happens to be a real estate agent. They have known him for a long time, and they tell him that they have found a house that they want to purchase.

"They ask him if he will write-up an offer for them on the home. He does so.

"The other agent, a few days later, calls the buyers to see if they want to do anything about the house. They say no.

"Afterward, they purchase the home through their friend, and he is paid a commission.

"Does anyone see anything wrong with this?" the old gentleman asks the audience through kind, squinting eyes.

An argument ensues in the audience as he polishes his glasses.

"Yes, I do," says one woman. "The buyers lied."

Nervous laughter breaks out. The speaker smiles, commenting that the buyers cannot be prosecuted.

"What about the agents?" he asks, replacing his glasses. "Is everything OK?"

"I don't see anything wrong," says another individual. "The second agent sold them the house and so he deserves the commission."

"How many people," asks the speaker, "feel that there is nothing wrong in this example--please raise your hands."

Half of the audience raises their hands.

A debate again develops, some people siding with the first agent, others siding with the second.

What is the setting for this meeting? A recent spring day at one of the largest local realty boards in the country, representing 1% of national membership.

Of the hands that were <u>not</u> raised, these are mostly tenured real estate agents. Some are joining this local board to expand their businesses, desiring access to properties and publications in more than one vicinity. Others have recently moved here and are joining to conduct their main business. Most of the new agents who did not raise their hands have had extensive business training.

The entire audience is comprised of the same mix of individuals that was described in the chapter titled "In Reality...": some are professionals, some have tremendous cross-business training. Most, however, are or have neither.

Earlier, before the speaker stepped onto the stage, another speaker had commented about the direct correlation between education and success in the industry. The higher the education, the higher the income. Interestingly, no one in the audience was observed to be taking notes during any part of the discussions.

The other half of the audience--who did not raise their hands--is made up mostly of new recruits and a few unsure veterans. New recruits who are required, just like the veterans, to attend this three-hour orientation meeting in order to join this local realty board.

The white-haired gentleman mentions that this same division of hands splits about the same way at each lecture. He says that he is always saddened to see how many people do not perceive a clear violation of one of the most basic and important codes of conduct in the real estate industry. The example constitutes one of the most flagrant violations and frequent complaints that is reviewed by his Committee.

"But the agent didn't know," someone in the audience protests, "that the buyers had been working with someone else. The buyers never told him."

"But how," wonders the speaker, "do you think the buyers came to view the house in the first place? Did someone show it to them? Certainly, the door did not magically open."

"And shouldn't the agent," he continues, "have known enough to ask his friends how they came to find that particular home?"

The speaker suggests later that as many people as possible volunteer to be on the Grievance Committee. That way, he duly notes, they will learn more about real estate than by practicing it, as he says he has done in his 35-year career.

He also strongly recommends that everyone quickly attend the mandatory course on Ethics and Agency Relationships currently required within 18 months in this specific state.

New recruits. Flying blindly. Seat-of-the-pants ethics. Not knowing right from wrong...

And many of these agents will be knocking on your door, calling you on the phone, advising you about "right" and "wrong" properties, ways to buy and sell, ways to do business... within the week.

As this 35-year veteran notes--this knowledge level is common among audiences that he sees twice a month, every month, year in and year out...

The auditorium is a beautiful room. It could comfortably seat 100. It is modern, plush, carpeted. The seats feel luxurious. The entire room looks and smells new. It also contains a 50+ inch color television for viewing films, a few of which were shown on other topics during this orientation. The room sparkles.

The auditorium is only one small part of a building that is owned by the local realty board. The rest of the building is similar in quality.

Each year the local, state and national boards collect dues which continue to support the system. The dues pay for the auditoriums, the large number of staff, the brochures, the services, the research centers, the legal hotlines, the political lobbyists, the campaign contributions...

All of these expenditures are furthered by a dream. By hope. By inspiration. By belief. In free enterprise and the system.

And by the scent of easy money?

For some people, dreams are the things reality is made of...

What would happen if half of the people in the audience--the half who raised their hands out of sheer ignorance, like half the hands at every meeting--were to disappear suddenly, being required to correct their errors in judgment before receiving membership? By how much would membership monies dwindle?

In defense of the industry, many people would say that the system is self-regulating because these new recruits immediately become the responsibility of the insured veteran brokers for whom they work--that the agency where the new people will be "employed" is required to help monitor behavior.

A neat and tidy argument. But as you have read in other sections of this book, the defense is a sham.

First, sales agents are not even given the status of "employee" in the industry. They are treated as less, much less.

Second, the broker and the agency are in business to make money, not to regulate behavior. There is more incentive to look the other way if a dollar can be pocketed than to forgo the money and to right a wrong.

Third, and most important, no veteran or manager can follow a new recruit around on every transaction. There just isn't enough time to hold the hand and to guide the mind of every agent.

Fourth, it is not simply the new recruits who know whether to raise their hands. Or who care to.

In a few short hours after this meeting, everyone in attendance will be a member of the local, state and national boards.

How can a self-policing organization allow half of its members to join and pay dues--when the members do not know the difference between right and wrong? Why are these people, in some instances, allowed 18 months to correct their deficiencies in judgment?

Is it any wonder why so many people have come forward and contributed stories to help document this book? To share personal experiences from otherwise innocent citizens who have been duped through the hearsay of uninformed real estate agents?

To obtain the highest designation in the industry of *broker*, one must be versed in ethics, agency relationships, finance, accounting, escrows, business administration, basic construction, and many other odds and ends.

Why don't these newcomers have the same knowledge?

Would it make life easier for the broker who accepts many of them as agents?

Would it possibly decrease the number of clear-cut industry violations?

Would it protect you, the consumer, from some of the mistakes that occur daily throughout the country?

Would it decrease the high costs of insurance in the industry for the gross errors and omissions that occur *hourly*?

Raising the education requirements might not eliminate fraud and deceit in the industry, but it is certainly a start.

When those 50% of new members know the difference between right and wrong and the ramifications of their behavior <u>before</u> they join their local real estate boards, then the industry will be taking the first step in protecting you, the consumer.

And every seasoned agent who doesn't raise a hand at meetings like these will sleep better at night knowing that the industry is elevating its standards.

Until then, these uninformed agents may as well be demonstrating vacuum cleaners or pots and pans at your local department store.

That is the consensus among the seasoned veterans, most of whom express nothing but contempt when they see brand new agents joining their offices.

For they know that they, too, like the industry, will suffer.

At the expense of you, the consumer.

ABOLISH THE "SLAVE SYSTEM"

For years brokers have fought tooth-and-nail to maintain access to the largest pool of unpaid labor despite its consequences--the most important being guaranteed nightmares for the general public.

As mentioned in the chapter titled "In Reality...," a new sales agent passes a licensing examination believing that real estate is a most noble profession steeped in law and tradition, where one can serve mankind while earning a very comfortable living.

But unlike a high school diploma or a college degree, a new agent cannot simply open the want ads in a newspaper and hope to find a job where one will be compensated, regardless of how humble the initial salary. Instead, most agents solicit local realty firms where they are usually invited to serve an apprenticeship without pay while learning "the business."

The new agent is not considered an employee. No pay, no benefits, no insurance. Simply an unpaid "slave" until the first commission is earned.

And what is "the business"? For a new agent this can mean answering phones, photocopying, typing ad copy, running errands, doing "floor time" (i.e., answering questions for the general public during assigned hours), showing properties for a senior agent, "sitting" open houses for other agents, opening a home for a home inspector...

In short, the new agent performs many extraneous duties during "training." And what, one may ask, is the agent training for?

What about law? What about finance? What about the construction of a home? Isn't this "product knowledge"?

The agent must take a class elsewhere in such topics to supplement one's education. In the meantime, the agent will learn the fundamentals of standard paperwork, contracts, and the inventory of available homes. And, of course, beginning sales techniques.

Finance and law are left to trained minds within the firm, or to outside consultants. And home construction? Who needs it? All one needs to know is the current inventory. *"Selling"* is more important than protecting a consumer's interests.

Armed and dangerous, where "a little knowledge is a dangerous thing," the new agent becomes desperate to unleash any tactic found in several earlier chapters that will result in a sale and--income.

Imagine, if you will, IBM in the 1960s. What if the IBM salesforce did not have product knowledge? How many IBM Selectric Typewriters would have been returned to the company because they did not perform like the personal computers that arrived twenty years later, as the starving salespeople might have promised? How many lawsuits would have been covered by IBM's "Errors and Omissions Insurance"? How would the company have thrived? Would you put faith in such a company?

What are the alternatives for the real estate industry? Either:

> a) compensate new agents during the training period, or

> b) increase the licensing requirements to expedite the
> training process, thereby protecting the public.

There is probably not one broker in the country who would volunteer for suggestion A.

Aside from the money issue, even the best firms experience the notorious problem of giving outstanding training and then having a new agent jump to another firm with a better commission structure immediately afterward.

Some firms try to circumvent this problem by combining training with mentor programs. The new agent works, eats and breathes with a senior agent, gaining valuable experience in live situations on real transactions. The new agent is not compensated. The senior agent, for all the time and trouble, will usually receive half of the new agent's commissions on the first three deals.

By then, the new agent is considered "seasoned," although training requirements in the industry are on-going.

In this way, the new agent gains more beneficial experience than the myriad facts memorized for the licensing exam.

But what is the difference between a broker and a new agent?

Answer: the agent is usually "broke" after the first few months in the business.

No one prepares a new agent for the six-month starvation period after earning a license. And then, it is more important to learn tactics to survive "on the street" than to "waste time" training on topics such as escrows.

If the agent were simply writing an insurance policy--then the bad transactions that constantly surface could be remedied with the stroke of a pen. But how does the normal consumer take a house back to the broker and ask for a refund?

It is time to both:

> a)   pay the "slaves," and
> b)   elevate the standards.

This is not the only answer to this problem. There still exists the chore of policing those unethical people who occasionally surface at, for example, 100% commission offices. In these agencies, each person pays a fixed fee for agency services, and then receives 100% of the commission earned. These people, if they are hungry, have too much incentive to violate proper practices.

In all fairness, "bad apples" can crop up at any agency, regardless of tenure in the business. The next major recommendation after this one addresses pertinent ideas for improving this situation.

Regardless, it is time to emancipate the "slaves."

When will the industry wake up and adopt practices such as "draw against commission"?

A study of companies in other industries across the country demonstrates that many adopt the policy of advancing monies to their salespeople in order to:

> a)   protect the salesperson in lean times, and
> b)   discourage unethical behavior which will later damage the firm.

Item B is critical.

Raising standards and fostering good people will only improve the industry and help you, the consumer.

ESTABLISH INDEPENDENT INVESTIGATIVE AGENCIES

Police normally do not like to investigate fellow police officers. It is human nature to believe in a person's goodness, especially if an individual has recited an oath "to protect and to serve" the community. Similarly, the real estate industry attempts to protect its own, giving a licensee the benefit of doubt until a complaint has been proven to be true. But unlike the police department, there are more incentives for realty boards to ignore complaints of the public.

Police departments are run on tax dollars. They have some public accountability. If a police officer violates an oath and must be discharged, there are more officers to take one's place, although morale may suffer. There are still tax dollars to hire or substitute other officers, although this process may take time.

In most communities, a real estate licensee joins a local realty board that attempts to maintain "law and order" among its members. Its members pay dues. Licensing fees. Annual board membership fees. Multiple listing service fees. And boards sell lockboxes to agents to place on the front doors of homes for sale. Boards lease lockbox keys. And they sell signs for the agents along with many other products. If a broker or agent has a license revoked, what happens to those fees? Sales decrease. The local board thus has incentive to overlook violations.

Let's look at two dramatic, everyday case examples which demonstrate the serious ramifications of this structure.

Case examples 385 and 1659:

Seller Tom had listed his home for sale with an agent of Firm M. The house sat on the market for a few months during the holidays, and then a buyer appeared. She wrote an offer, which, after some negotiation, was accepted. Then, like most scared new buyers, she asked for advice from a "friend."

The "friend" was also an agent of Firm M. The "friend" told her not to buy the house, and told her that he could get her a better deal elsewhere. Nothing could have been further from the truth. But alas, the transaction was cancelled.

Tom, also a real estate licensee, complained to his agent and to Firm M. He threatened to sue. The broker had violated the fiduciary responsibility. Tom threatened to petition to have the interfering agent's license revoked. And clearly, it should have been.

The firm hemmed and hawed. It could not patch together Tom's transaction. The buyer was no longer interested in the property. And, as Firm M safely asserted, the buyer had cancelled the contract based upon allowable contingencies, which were within the buyer's rights. It would be difficult to prove otherwise in court.

Fortunately, another buyer surfaced in the next few weeks to placate Tom by purchasing the property. But Tom, a good citizen, nevertheless filed a complaint against the interfering agent with the local realty board.

Tom filed all the necessary papers. And the board lost them. After the second filing and three days before the expiration of the deadline to prove the complaint, the local board contacted Tom. They said that they had been trying to contact him for a long time. Where had he been? They needed to investigate and/or prove the charges. Where was he? Wasn't he responsible? They had tried to contact him and had left messages, but he was not available... All of it untrue. In disgust, Tom dropped the complaint and moved to another city after his home closed escrow.

This is not one isolated case. This is a typical example. The point: the realty board does not have incentive to investigate itself for the sake of the public because it would lose its membership base--and hence its income.

Consider further ramifications of this problem...

Seller W had a speculative home in default, very close to foreclosure. He was also unemployed. His "friend," agent Len, volunteered to "help" W with the property. How? He suggested that W list his house with him immediately to try to sell it quickly. He also suggested that W come to work for him as an assistant, using his real estate license.

W did as Len suggested. The home was priced very low, but did not sell fast because it was tenant-occupied and difficult to show.

Each time W drafted an assistant-contract to define the pay, hours and duties as specified by Len, Len changed the terms and conditions. Meanwhile, W worked for Len in good faith for several weeks, answering calls, distributing Len's brochures, etc. Len kept promising that the pay would come.

Finally, noticing that W seemed to be getting distressed, the office manager approached W, asking him about business. He told her. The manager was horrified, and complained to her superiors and to the owner of the firm.

It turned out that Len was in no position to pay any kind of salary. He was having rough financial times himself. It was later learned that he had simply tried to price the home low enough to earn a commission, thus "solving" W's problem--and one of his own.

W protested. The listing contract was cancelled by the broker.

Len was not discharged from the firm.

Less than a week later, another incident occurred. A different agent asked Len about the zoning of one of his listings. The property was zoned R-4, or for multi-family use. Len instructed the agent to tell potential buyers that it was zoned single-family in order to avoid worry over possible apartment development, saying that the area was in the process of being down-zoned. With this blatant misrepresentation, the agent felt very uncomfortable. She complained to management. Len was still not discharged.

These are only two examples out of many that occurred with Len. He was not discharged because he was a reasonably good producer at the firm, and it was during a recession. The owner needed the money that Len brought into the company. If Len were discharged, he would simply go to another firm or to a 100% commission agency, carrying with him his same bag of unethical tricks.

W found out all of this after his listing was cancelled. How could W protest this treatment? There were several witnesses, and evidence existed in writing.

But if the firm sanctioned Len's behavior, what chance did W have? If the firm had incentive to retain Len, regardless of the risk, how much incentive did the local board have to prosecute an ethics violation?

All because there did not exist an independent investigative agency...

It is time to divorce the administrative bodies and their functions. The hand that points the finger, that maintains the "long arm of the law," should not be the one to control the purse.

There will always be those who attempt to take advantage of others. No perfect system exists. The controls for regulating behavior, however, are skewed toward protecting the industry, not the complainant.

And the one who pays is you, the consumer.

EPILOGUE

THE PRESENT

&

THE FUTURE

Those who cannot remember the past

are condemned to repeat it.

- Santayana, *Life of Reason*

THE PRESENT

The beginning of this book shows you that the residential real estate industry sets very high ideals. Lofty aspirations are meant to guide behavior, as well as obligations that, if not followed, are subject to disciplinary action.

Throughout the remainder of the book, you meet a variety of agents--from the exalted to the base. While many of the cases are not representative of all the honest agents who are available, one fact becomes clear: the forces of reality and human nature are much more powerful than the controls the industry has set in place to enforce its ideals.

Consequently, the industry resembles an auditorium containing many people who wish to quit smoking. And the people directing the efforts are like the leaders of the tobacco industry...

For we have met many in these pages who, perhaps like yourself, innocently seek the advice of a qualified professional to help them through one of the largest, most critical transactions of their lives. Rather than obtaining aid, many people are victimized by some of the hucksters who enter the business each year. And many others are victimized by people who have been in the industry for a long time, by veterans who continually practice scams, preying upon the weak. Some victims seek retribution, but justice is neither swift nor strong.

To this end, this text has been written. To protect the weak from the con artists, to show agents why a large part of the general public holds them in low esteem, and to demonstrate to the industry why it merits an unfavorable reputation.

But no book ever rose up to serve as one's shield.

The many people who contributed their stories here all expressed that similar detrimental circumstances would not befall others. For this reason, the book is organized into principles that may serve you as a reference through the Table of Contents during any of your residential real estate transactions.

The industry can never protect every consumer. The forces of greed and survival will always seek to exploit others. But with this book, you can begin to protect yourself...

THE FUTURE

There will always be errors in the real estate business. With the rapid development of information technologies, however, the future of real estate will bring forth increased mechanization and less human interaction.

Let's look at a scenario where people buy and sell homes in the future. Let's advance you to the year 2103. Shazamm!

Through your local communications link, you access the home shopping network, formally known as the Regional Domicile Grid or "RDG" in 22nd century parlance.

For each successful transaction, the RDG pockets a fee of 3%. Consumers, feeling frustrated for centuries with no standard commission structure, mandated that these fees be fixed. All fees and transactions are therefore set and regulated by government decree.

The RDG asks you a series of questions. For each, many options are given. You are shown pictures, color schemes, room dimensions, areas of town... You are asked to rank preferences for different options. For example, would you prefer two parking spaces and beige walls, or two parking spaces and peach colored walls... The RDG assigns weightings to these rankings in addition to gathering standard information regarding desired square footage, number of bedrooms, number of bathrooms, price, style, number of fireplaces...

After determining your profile, the RDG matches your preferences and income level to available domiciles that rank high according to your needs. For example, it locates a condominium with a "72" rating. Then it locates another with a "92" rating. The model indicates that you will prefer the latter domicile.

The RDG then gives you the addresses of the top five domiciles for which your income qualifies. You are left to view them on your own. In this way, the "X" factor is compensated because it is always unpredictable: the human factor.

Welcome to 2103.

Buyers never meet sellers. "Agents" are completely regulated. The "market" is now efficient. Information is quickly accessed and immediately updated. It is near-perfect. And "the market" is very predictable...

END NOTE

TI FINANCIAL is presently collecting information to be included in the following works:

GAMES DOCTORS PLAY

GAMES LAWYERS PLAY

GAMES INSURANCE AGENTS PLAY

If you have a true story pertinent to these topics that you would like considered for publication, please send your story to:

TI FINANCIAL
Research Department
Box 5503
Sherman Oaks, CA 91413-5503